Praise for *The Triangle Hold Encyclopedia*

I first trained with Steve Scott when I was training to win the Missouri State Championships and then the US Junior Nationals, the US Senior Nationals, and the US Open and World Championships. He knows matwork like God knows the Bible. No matter your level of experience, from white belt to white-haired sensei, you'll learn something from this book.

—Dr. AnnMaria Rousey De Mars
World and Pan American Games judo champion,
US national judo champion, US Olympic Festival champion,
7th degree black belt

As a combat sports television commentator, I continually find myself going back to my foundation of technical ground fighting and submission holds knowledge, which was originally established by Steve Scott. It's with great pride that I can claim Steve as both my first coach and my long-time friend. Quite simply, the man is both a legend and an encyclopedia. This new book vividly illustrates what those of us who are Steve Scott acolytes have long known.

—Sean Wheelock
experienced television commentator in combat sports,
ranging from MMA to Muay Thai

The Triangle Hold Encyclopedia is the "Triangle Bible" for all combat sport athletes. Steve Scott has literally written the book(s) on all aspects of judo that can be used in any combat sport, and this book is a quality guide to all aspects of the technique anyone can use and learn from.

The Triangle Hold Encyclopedia is a complete guide to the triangle technique. It covers entries [for holds] from every angle, [contains] many photos, and [offers] thorough explanations of every move. It is the perfect guide to apply the triangle from any position or situation you find yourself in during combat sports competition. If you already use this move, you will find the fine-tuning you may be lacking, and the triangle may become your go-to winning technique. A must-have for any combat sport competitor or coach.

Rest assured, many people will find this book a great addition to their library on judo and combat sports.

—Janet Trussell
World and Pan American Games sambo champion,
US national judo champion, US Olympic Festival champion,
4th degree black belt

Steve Scott's books have become a staple of my reference library, and *The Triangle Hold Encyclopedia* is no different. Steve has compiled a fantastic volume of techniques that reminds me how much more I still have to learn.

—Stephen Koepfer,
head coach of NY Combat Sambo,
SAG-AFTRA stunt performer for television and film, four-time
Team Combat Wrestling head coach, two-time Team
USA Sambo coach, author, martial artist

I have known Steve Scott for over three decades and in that time, he has come to be a very good friend. I've been involved in the martial arts/grappling sports for almost five decades, and Steve is one of the most knowledgeable coaches I have ever met. His new book, *The Triangle Hold Encyclopedia* is, in my opinion, the preeminent work on the subject. The genius of this book is that it is designed for grapplers of all styles, be it judo, sambo, jujitsu, or submission wrestling. The techniques are demonstrated with the gi/jacket as well as with no gi. There are clear descriptions and photographs demonstrating the techniques. Steve demonstrates not only the chokes, strangles, and arm bars from the triangle but also shows various entries to apply these techniques. I would encourage any grappler, regardless of style, who would like to improve their submission game to study this work.

—Gregg Humphreys,
judo/sambo coach, Dynamo Combat Club,
5th degree judo black belt, expert sambo in wrestling,
2nd degree black belt in Shingitai jujitsu,
North American representative for Igor Kurinnay's
Sambo for Professionals

The Triangle Hold Encyclopedia is a great addition to the other books Steve Scott has written. I really enjoyed *The Sambo Encyclopedia* and *The Juji Gatame Encyclopedia* and have been looking forward to this book. I often refer to these books while building the curricula for my own students.

This book does a great job detailing the development of the sankaku-jime. I'm a firm believer that understanding the history of the art better enables us to understand the purpose of the techniques we use and allows us to continue to take them even further for the next generation.

The information on the positional categories the triangle can be performed from is great for beginners through advanced practitioners. Also, those of us who are instructors should always be seeking the best approach to teaching techniques. This text gives great details that are easily passed on to our students. *The Triangle Hold Encyclopedia* is a must-have for your martial arts library regardless of your grappling style.

—Larry W. Keith,
professor, sensei, Kodokan judo sandan (3rd degree),
Brazilian jiu-jitsu black belt, author, and video creator;
instructing since 1994 and school owner since 2002

Triangle Hold Encyclopedia

Also by Steve Scott

The Judo Advantage
The Sambo Encyclopedia
Vital Jujitsu (with John Saylor)
Juji Gatame Encyclopedia
Winning on the Mat
Conditioning for Combat Sports (with John Saylor)
Tap Out Textbook
Groundfighting Pins and Breakdowns
Drills for Grapplers
Throws and Takedowns
Grappler's Book of Strangles and Chokes
Vital Leglocks
Championship Sambo: Submission Holds and Groundfighting
Championship Sambo (DVD)
Armlock Encyclopedia
Juji Gatame Complete (with Bill West)
Coaching on the Mat

Triangle Hold Encyclopedia

Comprehensive Applications for Triangle
Submission Techniques

By
Steve Scott

YMAA Publication Center
Wolfeboro, NH USA

YMAA Publication Center, Inc.
PO Box 480
Wolfeboro, New Hampshire, 03894
United States of America
1-800-669-8892 • info@ymaa.com • www.ymaa.com

ISBN: 9781594396496 (print) • ISBN: 9781594396502 (ebook)
Copyright © 2014, 2022 by Steve Scott
All rights reserved including the right of reproduction in whole or in part in any form.
Copy editor: Doran Hunter
Cover design: Axie Breen
Typesetting by Westchester Publishing Services
This book typeset in Adobe Caslon and Franklin Gothic

Illustrations courtesy of the author, unless otherwise noted.

20210501

Publisher's Cataloging in Publication

Names: Scott, Steve, 1952- author.

Title: The triangle hold encyclopedia : comprehensive applications for triangle submission techniques / by Steve Scott.

Description: Wolfeboro, NH USA : YMAA Publication Center, [2022] | "For all grappling styles"-- Cover. | Includes bibliographical references.

Identifiers: ISBN: 9781594396496 (print) | 9781594396502 (ebook) | LCCN: 2022931248

Subjects: LCSH: Wrestling holds--Handbooks, manuals, etc. | Wrestling holds--Training. | Wrestling-- Training. | Wrestling--Coaching--Handbooks, manuals, etc. | Hand-to-hand fighting, Oriental--Training. | Hand-to-hand fighting--Training. | Judo--Training. | Mixed martial arts--Training. | Martial arts--Holding--Training. | BISAC: SPORTS & RECREATION / Wrestling. | SPORTS & RECREATION / Martial Arts / General. | SPORTS & RECREATION / Health & Safety.

Classification: LCC: GV1196.4.H64 S36 2022 | DDC: 796.812--dc23

Editor's Note: Throughout this book, readers will see mention of US Judo, judo's national governing body. This organization is also known as US Judo, Inc. and USA Judo. For our purposes, the terms are synonymous.

Printed in Canada.

IN APPRECIATION

A sincere "thank you" goes to a lot of people who helped make this book possible. My publisher David Ripianzi and my editor Doran Hunter and the entire team at YMAA Publications have been supportive, encouraging, and professional in the development, production, and publication of this book as well as with all of my books that YMAA has published. As with all my other books, my wife Becky supplied her love, ideas, critical thought, and support during the process of writing this book and getting it to print. I don't deserve her, but I'm glad she's there.

The photography for this book was the result of the hard work and dedication of several professionals who gave selflessly of their time and talent. Mark Lozano, Terry Smemo, Sharon Vandenberg, Jorge Garcia, and Jake Pursley provided the photos used in this book and have my heartfelt thanks.

But this book could not have been produced had it not been for the Welcome Mat and Shingitai athletes and coaches who freely gave their talent and time to this project. They patiently posed for the photos but did more than that; they contributed their enthusiasm, experience, expertise, ideas, criticism, and talent. Derrick Darling, Dr. AnnMaria DeMars, Kelvin Knisely, Sandi Harrelson, Mike Pennington, Jarrod Fobes, Jeff Owens, William Cook, Ben Goehrung, Jake Pursley, Eric Millsap, J. T. Thayne, Steve Potter, James Rippee, Ken Jarnigan, Dre Glover, Eric McIntosh, Aric Weaver, T. J. Barnet, Bill West, Anthony Ishmael, J. P. Pocock, Kreig Jarnigan, Wes Wassmer, Justin Metcalf, Brian Hanson, and Josh Wyrick have my sincere thanks for appearing in the photos in this book.

Contents

Part 3: Triangle Chokes   97

Part 4: Triangles   151

Part 5: Triangle Chokes   189

Part 6: Prevention, Defenses, and Escapes   231

Part 7: Epilogue   261

INTRODUCTION

The legs are powerful tools that a grappler in any combat sport can, and should, use to his or her advantage. But as important as the power of the legs may be, knowing how to use that power is even more important and that's what this book is about. What has come to be known as the triangle choke has proven to be the best use of a grappler's legs when it comes to strangling an opponent in any kind of fight.

The purpose of this book is to explore what makes a successful triangle choke and many of the applications and variations that make this one of the most effective strangling techniques in any fighting sport. As with any realm of technical study, not every application or variation of the triangle choke can be presented in these pages. However, in this book we will present and examine many of them.

This book will emphasize the triangle chokes and other strangling techniques using the legs. Some grapplers or jujitsu exponents include what is known as an "arm triangle" as another method of triangle chokes. While these techniques are effective, this book will focus on the legs and lower body as the primary tools to perform the triangle choke. Some exponents use the term arm triangles, while others (this author included) categorize these type of chokes as "shoulder chokes" or *kata jime* (shoulder choke) and in some cases even "shoulder holds" or *kata gatame*. Not including the arm triangles in this book in no way diminishes these techniques or the people who classify them as triangle chokes. It's simply this author's method of coaching and categorizing triangle chokes.

A central characteristic of this book is that the skills presented on these pages can be used in a variety of fighting and grappling sports. It is the author's firm belief that a good choke is a good choke no matter who does it, in what context or sport it is used, or who invented it. Some chokes presented in this book may not be suitable for certain grappling sports, but every attempt has been made to present the skills in this book so that as many people as possible can make use of as many chokes as possible in as many situations as possible.

As a coach and author, I hope that the concepts and skills presented here will impel you, the reader, to develop your abilities to the best possible level. If you are successful, then I am successful.

Steve Scott

"If you don't know how you got somewhere, you don't know where you are."
James Burke

Part 1: The Triangle Choke
How It Got To Be What It Is Today

James Burke's adaptation of an old mariner's saying certainly applies to the subject of this chapter (as well as to the entire book). Another way of saying it for our purposes might be that if we don't have some factual idea of how the triangle choke developed and evolved over the years, we won't appreciate its capacity as a functional weapon or its versatility as a tool that can be used in any fighting sport.

A HISTORY OF THE TRIANGLE CHOKE

When Prof. Jigoro Kano developed Kodokan judo in 1882, he set the stage for the growth, evolution, and expansion not only of his brilliant invention, Kodokan judo, but for what has come to be known as martial arts in general. It was the exponents of Prof. Kano's judo (as well as Prof. Kano himself) who developed the concepts of combat sports that would expand to a variety of offshoots throughout the world.

It was because of this technical experimentation, innovation, development, and growth that the concept of controlling an opponent with the legs, and then using the legs as a weapon to strangle an opponent, came into being.

In the years before Prof. Kano founded his judo, what we now know as triangle chokes were not used to any degree at all. The feudal jujutsu of Japan was designed for fighting and usually fighting an armed opponent on a battlefield. There is little, if any, historical mention of strangling an opponent with the legs in any of the ancient or feudal documents chronicling the various jujutsu ryu (schools). Grappling with an enemy combatant and exposing the legs or lower extremities to a knife or sword wasn't a wise thing to do for the *bujin* (warriors) of that time.

So, it wasn't until the "sporting" concept of grappling was introduced to the Japanese culture through judo that such techniques as *sankaku* (or *sangaku*) *jime* (triangle strangles) were developed and used. The Kosen judo exponents of the early 1900s who specialized in the groundfighting aspect of judo contributed a great deal to the early development of triangle and leg chokes. This led to a greater appreciation of triangle chokes among the top Kodokan judo fighters who spread the word outside of Japan to an international audience.

Historically, the roots of what came to be known as *katame waza* (holding or grappling techniques) or *newaza*

(groundfighting techniques starting from a supine position—what is now commonly called the guard) originate from a school that was a rival to Kodokan in its early years around the turn of the twentieth century. The exponents of *Fusen-ryu* jujutsu proved superior to the Kodokan fighters in an early dual tournament (in 1900) and it didn't take long for Jigoro Kano to bring in Mataemon Tanabe, the headmaster of the Fusen school, to teach his students at the Kodokan Judo Institute. Additionally, Prof. Kano recruited exponents of another school of jujutsu that placed emphasis on groundfighting, the *Jikishin-ryu*, around the same time to instruct his Kodokan pupils. This period, from 1900 to 1906, saw a marked improvement in the quality of groundfighting among the Kodokan judo exponents. Notably, in 1906, Prof. Kano finalized his work on *katame no kata* (form of grappling) to complement the already-existing *nage no kata* (form of throwing). These two structured forms of learning technical skills formed the basis of the early teaching of judo at the Kodokan. Several of the Kodokan's top instructors, notably Hajime Isogai, Tsunetane Oda, and Yaichibei Kanemitsu (among others) formed what was known as Kansai judo, a group of Kodokan instructors who developed the groundfighting of judo to a higher level in an attempt to be on par with the highly refined throwing techniques of Kodokan judo.

This group, as well as others, developed the Kosen judo movement that placed emphasis on newaza and was popular among preparatory and high school students as well as university students from 1914 to 1943.

It was in the early days of Kosen judo that sangaku (or sankaku) jime (the triangle strangle or choke) was initially developed. Historians differ somewhat as to who exactly was the originator of sankaku jime, but it was the work of Oda, Isogai, and Kanemitsu that laid the technical foundation that saw the development of the triangle choke.

When Mitsuo Maeda introduced Kodokan judo to Brazil (and in particular to the Gracie family) in the 1920s, he set in motion the eventual development and evolution of Brazilian jiu-jitsu and their approach to grappling. The Brazilian exponents took a particular liking to the triangle choke and (independently of the Kodokan and Kosen judo movements) developed their own approach to the study and teaching of the triangle choke as a distinct and functional tool in grappling and fighting, especially when applied from the bottom newaza (guard) grappling position.

As mentioned before, the concept of "newaza" was (and continues to be) a major aspect of not only Kosen judo but also the general approach to grappling on the mat or ground used in Kodokan judo and Brazilian jiu-jitsu. And this approach to fighting off of the buttocks or back led to the early development of *sankaku jime* (as well as a variety of other skills) in a highly complex and functionally effective way. As previously mentioned, the early (and current) proponents of Brazilian jiu-jitsu focused on this grappling position and have done much for the further technical development of the triangle choke as an effective weapon.

STRANGLING IS THE GREAT EQUALIZER

Strangles and chokes are the "great equalizer" in any form of fighting, whether in a self-defense situation, law enforcement or military applications, or in any of the fighting sports. Smaller or physically weaker fighters can (and do) defeat larger, stronger opponents with chokes and strangles. Depriving an opponent or assailant of the ability to breathe will make even the strongest men surrender (or pass out). If someone has forced his opponent to submit or surrender from a strangle, the fight is over and everyone knows who the winner is, since forcing an opponent to choke, sputter, gag, or go unconscious leaves no doubt who won the fight. It's rarely a fluke when one fighter forces his opponent to give up from a choke. Maybe someone can score a "lucky punch" or a "fluke throw," but it's very rare to score a lucky or fluke choke on an opponent. Often, a strangling technique is the result of one grappler or fighter controlling the position of his opponent and methodically working to make the strangle effective. In many cases, a physically smaller or weaker fighter may be able to choke his larger and stronger opponent, forcing the larger fighter to submit or go unconscious.

Chokes and strangles are probably the subtlest of all fighting or grappling skills. It's okay to be sneaky when doing chokes or strangles. In fact, it's an asset. A good strangler knows how to use his hands, arms, feet, legs, or any part of his body to manipulate and control an opponent. A good strangler seems almost relaxed or "loose" but is always gripping, grabbing, holding, or controlling some part of his opponent's body so that he can ultimately strangle him into submission. A good strangler has a "feel" as to how to use his hands, arms, feet, legs, and other body parts independently of each other, but working together to get the job done.

The *"shime waza"* (strangling techniques), initially conceived and developed in Japanese fighting arts such as jujutsu and Kodokan judo, gave sport grappling a whole new dimension. In Japanese fighting and grappling in the early twentieth century, the theory of shime waza was an integral concept in fighting or grappling on the ground. What may have been considered "dirty wrestling" in Western forms of grappling or wrestling in the late 1800s and into the early 1900s was considered just another way of gaining an advantage over an opponent to the Japanese.

TRIANGLE CHOKES: AN EXPLANATION OF SANKAKU JIME

The method we recognize as sankaku jime or the triangle choke was (as mentioned previously) initially conceived and developed by the Japanese. To begin to understand this form of strangling an opponent, let's look at the translation from the original Japanese. The word "san" means "three." The word "kaku" means "corner" or "angle." Thus, "san-kaku" is translated to "three cornered" or "triangle." The word "jime" is an adaptation of the word "shime." The "sh" is hardened to "j" when used as a suffix in the Japanese language. The word "shime" means "to tighten," "to squeeze," "to constrict," or "to shut or close." In common usage, "shime" translates to "strangle by squeezing or tightening." We could call this choke the "three-cornered squeeze" but that is too cumbersome and doesn't do this great weapon justice. Simply calling it the triangle choke seems to make the most sense.

A triangle choke takes place anytime the legs of the attacker are wrapped around his opponent at the neck area in a triangle or figure four (that has been formed by the attacker's legs and feet) and the attacker applies pressure to the neck, strangling his opponent. What is often called a triangle choke is a leg choke with the attacker forming a triangle with his legs and using the power of his legs to strangle or choke his opponent. Strangling an opponent with the strength of the legs produces some of the most powerful submission techniques ever invented or used in sport combat.

This entire book is devoted to the basic concept of a fighter or grappler wrapping his legs and feet tightly around his opponent's neck, head, and arm and strangling him with the strength of the attacker's legs.

TRIANGLE CHOKES: A VARIETY OF APPLICATIONS

This book presents a comprehensive analysis of triangle chokes and the many applications, variations, set ups, and positions from which they are applied. Additionally, defenses and escapes are examined, and there will be discussion of how to systematically teach and study triangle chokes so they become an effective part of every fighter or grappler's arsenal.

TRAPPING THE OPPONENT'S HEAD/NECK, SHOULDER, AND ARM IN THE TRIANGLE

Presented here are some examples of how the attacker uses the triangle he has formed with his feet and legs to either trap the opponent's head/neck, shoulder, and arm to create the strangling action or to trap only the opponent's head to create the strangling action. Both are valid triangle chokes, but the "head only" triangle choke is not allowed in some forms of sport combat, so make sure of the rules before you use it.

Trapping Opponent's Head/Neck, Shoulder, and Arm

EXAMPLE #1

This photo shows an example of a basic triangle choke from the bottom guard position. Look at how the bottom grappler has formed a triangle with his feet and legs so that he is trapping his opponent's head (and neck), shoulder, and arm.

Trapping Opponent's Head

EXAMPLE #1

This photo shows an example of a basic triangle choke from the bottom guard position, but in this situation, the bottom grappler traps only his opponent's head in his triangle. Depending on the rules of the combat sport, this application may not be allowed, but it's still a strong choke and has the added benefit of being a nasty headlock as well.

Trapping Opponent's Head/Neck, Shoulder, and Arm

EXAMPLE #2

This photo shows a triangle choke from a top controlling position where the attacker traps his opponent's head (and neck) along with his shoulder and arm to create a strong choke.

Trapping Opponent's Head

EXAMPLE #2

This photo shows a position that is almost exactly the same as the previous photo, but the attacker does not trap his opponent's arm or shoulder and traps his head only. This is a strong choke as well as an effective neck lock.

THE LEG SCISSORS AND ITS DESCENDENT: THE TRIANGLE

While this book focuses on triangles, a few words on the scissors hold are included here to provide some insight from both a technical point of view and an historical point of view.

Any fan of professional wrestling will recognize a scissors hold. This is probably the oldest form of applying pressure to an opponent's head, neck, or body used in any style of grappling or wrestling. Some people (this author included) believe that the triangle hold with the legs is an offshoot of the original scissors hold with the legs and is the historical forerunner of the triangle hold or choke. It's also interesting to note that in just about any style of wrestling from any culture around the world, the scissors hold has been used for centuries.

Technically, when a grappler or wrestler wraps his legs around any part of his opponent's body or head, hooks his ankles or lower legs together, and then applies pressure by squeezing or constricting (or even simply holding the opponent without applying pressure), that is a "scissors." An adaptation of the scissors hold is the subject of this book, the triangle. When the attacker uses his feet and legs to form a triangle or "figure four" around any part of his opponent's body or head and then control or apply pressure (or simply to hold the opponent), that is a "triangle." Generally, a triangle hold is more effective in both applying pressure and controlling an opponent, but a scissors hold can be effective as well, depending on the circumstances and rules or the match or fight.

As with the triangle, a scissors can be used to apply pressure to an opponent's head or neck as well as his body so that he submits from the pressure. A scissors hold can also be used to control an opponent so that the attacker can apply some other type of submission or finishing hold or technique.

This brings up the subject of the concept of "shime waza" (constricting or squeezing techniques) as developed by the early exponents of Kodokan judo. The idea behind shime waza was for the attacker to use any part of his body or appendages (as well as any part of his clothing such as a judogi) to apply so much pressure to an opponent that the opponent would either submit or go unconscious. Any part of the opponent's body was fair game, but eventually the rules of the sport of judo limited these attacks to the neck and throat of the opponent. Such moves as *dojime* (literally meaning, "body squeezing") were eventually prohibited and, through the years, the concept of shime waza was interpreted to mean "strangling techniques" or any attack directed at an opponent's throat.

In the photos that follow, some examples of the leg scissors are presented.

Using a Scissors Against an Opponent's Body

In what has come to be called the "closed guard," the bottom grappler squeezes his legs together, constricting the top grappler's torso. This is another example of what the Japanese call "dojime" or body constriction.

Another example of using the legs to scissor the opponent's torso with the intent of constricting him so hard that the opponent submits from the pain. These are just some of the many variations of using the legs to scissor an opponent.

Using the Scissors Against an Opponent's Head or Neck

This photo shows a basic application of the leg scissors applied on an opponent's head. The attacker squeezes his legs together; to quote John Saylor: "Squeeze his head so hard, it pops like a zit."

While the Japanese have been credited with the early development of the triangle hold or choke, the triangle also has historical roots in the Western style catch-as-catch-can wrestling that developed in Europe and the United States. When professional wrestling was a legitimate sport, using the legs to squeeze an opponent into submission was a popular way to end a match. The figure-four hold was a well-developed wrestling move that was used to control and apply pressure to the head, neck, body, arms, legs, and any body part that could be manipulated by an attacker's legs. Just as the Japanese developed the "triangle," the exponents of Western catch wrestling (and later amateur and freestyle wrestling) developed the figure-four hold within the confines of the rules of the wrestling where it was used. While the Japanese included choking techniques, the catch wrestlers of Europe and the United States used this move more as a headlock or neck pressure technique since "strangling" an opponent was against the rules in catch wrestling (although "sleeper holds" and other strangles were used extensively as well). Ed "Strangler" Lewis (among other prominent professional wrestlers) used the sleeper hold and figure-four headlock with great success in the early 1900s.

While we owe a debt of gratitude to the early catch wrestlers for their development of the figure four as a headlock, it was the Japanese Kodokan and Kosen judo exponents and later, the Brazilian jiu-jitsu exponents, who developed and refined the strangling technique that we now recognize as the triangle choke.

As Kodokan judo spread throughout the world during the course of the twentieth century and as Brazilian jiu-jitsu developed as an offshoot of Kodokan judo and would go on to become a recognized sport in its own right, a new fighting sport evolved from a number of different sources: mixed martial arts. Mixed martial arts (MMA) developed as a unique and distinct fighting sport, gaining huge popularity in the last decade of the twentieth century. Along with the technical innovations seen in MMA, a variety of submission grappling and submission wrestling styles emerged as well. All of this intense and eclectic interest in grappling and fighting sports has led to a wealth of innovative skills and training methods. If there was ever a "purist" point of view concerning the fighting sports or disciplines, it's sure not the case now. Because of this, there is an emphasis on functional and practical technical skills, and the development of the triangle choke has come from many different sources.

From the early development of sankaku jime in Kodokan and Kosen judo, to the contributions of the Brazilian jiu-jitsu exponents, the early professional wrestlers in catch-as-catch-can wrestling, and a diverse group of grapplers and fighters in the late twentieth and early twenty-first centuries, the triangle choke has evolved as one of the most popular techniques in any fighting sport.

So, for the purposes of understanding how the triangle choke has evolved and how it will continue to develop, it's best to say that it is an offspring with many parents from many parts of the world. This author hopes that this book will serve as a positive addition to the technical development of the triangle choke.

BODY TRIANGLES

Using a triangle hold on an opponent's body serves two primary purposes. The first purpose is to apply so much pressure on an opponent's torso or abdomen that he submits. The second purpose is to use the body triangle to control an opponent in order to apply a submission or finishing technique (such as a choke or other submission technique or, if in a fight or MMA match, to control the opponent in order to inflict punches or other types of striking techniques).

BODY TRIANGLE: MAKE THE OPPONENT SURRENDER

This photo shows the attacker using a body triangle with the intent of forcing his opponent to submit from the pressure applied to the abdomen or torso. This form of a body triangle is known, again, as "dojime" or "body squeezing" and is one of the original approaches to the concept of shime waza used in Kodokan judo (and Kosen judo). It was also used in Western catch wrestling with great success as a submission technique.

BODY TRIANGLE: CONTROL THE OPPONENT

This photo shows the attacker using a body triangle with the intent of controlling his opponent so he can apply another finishing technique (in this case, a rear naked choke). While the primary intent for the attacker is to control his opponent, he can still apply as much pressure as possible to force his opponent to surrender from the pressure applied from the body triangle as well as the other finishing or submission technique he chooses to use.

This photo shows the attacker using a body triangle from the bottom guard position to control his opponent. The bottom grappler can use this body triangle to apply pressure, but more often, he may use the body triangle to control his opponent so he can apply a variety of chokes or armlocks from this position.

TRIANGLE TO CONTROL OPPONENT'S LEGS

This photo shows how the top grappler can use a triangle with his legs to trap and control both of his opponent's legs as he pins him.

A better-known application is the "half guard." This takes place when one grappler traps one of the opponent's legs with either a triangle hold or a scissors hold. In this situation, the bottom grappler is using a half-guard along with a leg triangle to trap the top grappler's right leg.

TECHNICAL TIP: A leg triangle can be used to control just about any part of an opponent's body or head. The skills presented here are just some of the applications showing the versatility of the leg triangle and how it can be used as a viable tool to not only control an opponent, but to make him tap out.

AN ORGANIZED APPROACH

One of the functions on this book is to examine and then provide a systematic and organized approach to teaching and learning, then to practicing and ultimately using triangle chokes in functional and realistic ways. This book has been patterned after one of my other books published by YMAA Publication Center, *The Juji Gatame Encyclopedia*. In that book, I attempted to offer a logical methodology for the study and practice of the cross-body armlock as well as to provide specific practical, realistic, and functionally sound applications of that particular armlock. Similarly, the goal of this book is to offer both a wide range of functional applications and variations of the triangle choke and to provide a logical organizational structure that will supply a sound foundation for future learning and development.

Good organization answers a lot of questions and solves a lot of problems. It helps in providing a cohesive and systematic approach to learning. With this in mind,

this book is organized so that it presents the triangle choke from four distinct yet common situational positions. Each of these positions is unique, and while they sometimes tend to blend into each other (due to the fluid and changeable situations in a fight or match), these four starting positions provide a stable foundation from which a triangle choke can be successfully used in real-world situations.

But before we start, let's look at how triangle chokes have been traditionally classified.

THE HISTORICAL CLASSIFICATION OF TRIANGLE CHOKES

Historically, a loose classification of triangle chokes initially developed in Kosen judo (which was later accepted by Kodokan judo). This historical classification of the different forms of sankaku jime (triangle choke) featured four different identifiable finishing positions:

Omote sankaku jime (front or facing opponent triangle choke).

Yoko sankaku jime (side triangle choke).

Gyaku sankaku jime (reverse triangle choke).

This loose arrangement of the different forms and applications of the triangle choke has worked reasonably well but doesn't particularly account for all the variable positions from which triangle chokes are initially started and applied. These four basic classifications are based on how a triangle choke is ended or how it looks in its finished position. While this has provided a framework for what the triangle choke was supposed to look like when it was finished or applied, it didn't offer much clarification as to how the triangle choke was started or the position from which it was begun. The approach for classifying and explaining triangle chokes used in this book is based on the initial starting position with the intention of providing a systematic structure. Doing this allows for a more open-ended approach to the study and learning (as well as training) of triangle chokes, which offers a wider variety of functional setups and applications for this technique. So then, through this book, it's hoped that a more functional approach to classifying and ultimately teaching and learning triangle chokes will be adopted. For the purposes of how triangle chokes are functionally applied, this book will identify them in the following four categories:

Ura sankaku jime (rear triangle choke).

(1) TRIANGLE CHOKES FROM THE BOTTOM GUARD POSITION

These are triangles started when the attacker is in the bottom (guard) position or fighting off of the back or buttocks.

The bottom grappler will start his triangle choke from this standard bottom guard position with both grapplers engaged on the mat as shown.

An opponent who is standing and mobile faces the bottom grappler who may (among other things) attempt a triangle choke.

(2) TRIANGLE CHOKES FROM A BACK/SIDE RIDE OR CONTROLLING FROM THE OPPONENT'S BACK

This classification of triangles is started when the attacker is riding his opponent and has his opponent's back (as in a wrestler's ride, spiral ride, rodeo ride, or rear mount).

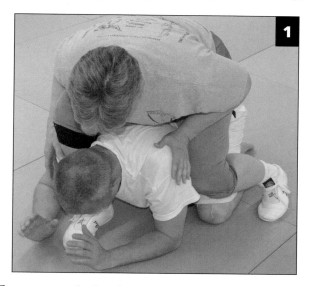

The top grappler has her opponent's back and will start her triangle choke from this position.

The top grappler is riding or controlling his opponent from the side and initiates his attack from this position.

The back grappler has a seated rodeo ride or rear mount and can initiate his triangle choke attack from this position.

(3) TRIANGLE CHOKES STARTING IN FRONT OF AN OPPONENT

These are triangles started when one or both grapplers are kneeling on one or both knees in a neutral position or when the attacker is positioned at the top of his opponent's head either on one knee (or both knees) or standing.

This photo shows both grapplers situated in a kneeling front neutral position; the attacker will initiate his attack from this position.

In some instances, the top grappler will be positioned in front of his opponent and at the top of his opponent's head as shown here. In this photo, both grapplers are kneeling on the mat.

In this photo, the top grappler is standing and his opponent is on all fours or on his knees on the mat. When the attacker attempts a jumping triangle choke, both grapplers may be in a standing position facing each other.

(4) TRIANGLE CHOKES STARTED FROM A PINNING OR HOLDING POSITION

These are triangles started when the attacker starts from a pinning position such as side control, front mount, leg press, scarf hold, or north-south pinning position. This is a broad range of starting positions with the common feature being that the attacker is controlling his opponent with the opponent primarily on his back or back/side.

The attacker is controlling his opponent directly from the side and can initiate his triangle attack from this side-control position.

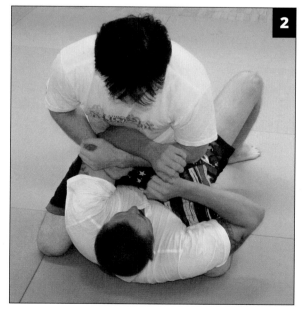

The attacker is controlling the bottom grappler with a mount as shown here and can start his triangle choke from this controlling position.

The attacker is controlling the bottom grappler from the side with a *kesa gatame* (scarf hold). From this position, the attacker can start his triangle choke.

The attacker is controlling his opponent with a north-south pin (*kami shiho gatame* or upper four-corner hold) and can initiate his triangle attack from this position.

The attacker is controlling his opponent with a leg press and can work to secure a *juji gatame* (cross-body armlock) or start a triangle choke from this position.

THE ANATOMY OF A STRANGLING TECHNIQUE AND A WORD OF CAUTION

The action of strangling may often (but not always) cause pain, especially when using the legs, and could have lethal consequences if applied long enough. That's why they used to hang bad guys in the Old West: it hurt and it was effective. Aside from that obvious point, cutting off the blood supply to the brain deprives the brain of oxygen and causes unconsciousness. The fact is, when you strangle or choke someone you are depriving him of his breath, and no matter how tough a guy is he still has to breathe. Apart from the physical effects, depriving someone of his ability to breathe has a big psychological impact on him.

You usually want to focus your choke on, or directly below, the Adam's Apple (thyroid cartilage). The thyroid cartilage is located right under the hyoid bone, a small bone that supports the thyroid cartilage and has many functions in swallowing. The trachea (windpipe) is located below the thyroid cartilage and is a flexible tube made up of cartilage. All these things are tough but not really made

for having somebody else squeeze them with great intensity! The sides of the neck contain the carotid arteries, which are large arteries and the brain's major source of blood. When they are constricted, most of the blood going to the brain doesn't get there anymore. Deprived of oxygen for even four or five seconds, the brain starts to shut down and unconsciousness occurs. If the brain is deprived of oxygen for four to six minutes, clinical death can occur. Whether you make an opponent pass out from constricting his carotid arteries or constricting his windpipe and connected organs, you still deprive him of oxygen.

Using strangles and chokes is serious business and is not for the immature. The author has coached for many years specializing in submission techniques and sincerely believes strangles and chokes are more dangerous than armlocks. A broken arm or leg can mend, but the effects of the brain cells lost from being choked cold always stay with you. The lack of oxygen to the brain kills brain cells and these brain cells don't grow back. Lose enough of them and neurological damage can take place.

It's better to tap out than pass out, especially in training. Don't be macho and risk serious injury and possible problems later in life. By the same token, if you're strangling an opponent or training partner and he taps out, he means it. Release the pressure and stop choking him for his safety. An old saying goes, "When in doubt, tap out." You're not any less brave, less tough, or less of anything. You're using your survival instinct to let your opponent know it's time to stop choking you. Don't risk your health or be a risk to the health of others. Practice safe and practice smart. It's better to tap out than pass out.

THE DIFFERENCE BETWEEN A STRANGLE AND A CHOKE

It's common to interchange the words "strangle" and "choke," and this book is no different. Specifically, "strangle" describes all the techniques we associate with any technique or move that attacks the neck or throat. "Choke" is more specific and refers to an action that obstructs or blocks the windpipe. Often, we refer to any strangle aimed against the side of the neck and the carotid arteries as just that, a strangle. Any strangle that closes, blocks, or obstructs the front of the neck at the throat is often referred to as a choke. A choke makes an opponent gag and sputter and is often more painful than when you cut off the blood supply to his brain pressing against his carotid arteries. But we all use the words "choke" and "strangle" to mean either action, so it really doesn't matter if you call it a "strangle" or a "choke"; we all know what is meant.

HOW TRIANGLE CHOKES WILL BE PRESENTED IN THIS BOOK

This book will present triangle chokes from the four basic starting positions shown earlier in this chapter. They are (1) triangle chokes starting from the bottom guard position. (2) Triangle chokes starting from in front of an opponent. (3) Triangle chokes starting from a rodeo ride or behind an opponent. (4) Triangle chokes starting from a pinning or holding position. Additionally, a chapter on the prevention, defense, and escapes for triangle chokes will be presented. Each chapter will start with an examination of the basic skills that are contained in that particular chapter and then go on to a presentation of the many functional and practical applications of triangle chokes.

Hopefully, in this way, the most thorough examination, analysis, and presentation of the core skills and many different applications of the triangle choke can be offered in the pages of this book.

While it may not be the case that every triangle choke ever devised appears in this book, a lot of them are presented here with the intention of spurring in-depth analysis, study, and innovation on the part of every reader. With this in mind, let's start.

Part 2: Triangle Chokes
From the Bottom Guard Position

TRIANGLES FROM THE BOTTOM GUARD POSITION

The oldest and most basic way of performing a triangle choke is when the attacker is on the bottom fighting from his buttocks, back, or backside. As a result, this position produces a large number of opportunities (and as a result a large number of applications) for a triangle choke.

Historically, and as mentioned earlier, fighting from the bottom in what is now commonly called the guard position has been known in Japanese judo (both Kodokan judo and its offshoot Kosen judo) as newaza (grappling techniques from a supine or reclining position). Japanese judo athletes, especially those who followed the Kosen form of judo where the emphasis was (and continues to be) on groundfighting, favored strangling techniques, and triangle chokes from the bottom were developed to a high standard. Likewise, Brazilian jiu-jitsu exponents have traditionally favored fighting from the newaza or guard position and have developed highly refined triangle chokes from this position. The triangle chokes applied from the bottom guard position have proved to be a mainstay in many modern forms of sport combat including MMA (mixed martial arts).

From a coaching perspective, initially presenting the fundamental skills of the triangle choke from the bottom guard position seems to be the most effective way to develop the technical skills necessary for effective triangle chokes from any starting position. This is what I do as a coach, and it has been my experience that athletes who initially learn triangle chokes from the bottom guard position gain a better fundamental understanding of what the triangle choke is about and ultimately progress in skill acquisition more quickly and develop a more disciplined approach to applying triangles from any position. Literally, the best way to learn triangle chokes is from the ground up.

The next few pages of this section analyze what makes the triangle choke from the bottom guard position work. After this, a variety of functional applications and variations are presented using triangles to control, trap, and choke an opponent. Not every variation of the triangle choke from the bottom guard position may be presented, but a good number are. Don't be afraid to take what you see on these pages and experiment, innovate, and create new applications and variations of the triangle choke.

TWO BASIC BOTTOM DIRECTIONAL POSITIONS OR ANGLES OF ATTACK

There are basically two directional applications for triangle chokes from the bottom guard. While there are any number of variations, the two most common come from when the attacker (the bottom grappler) is lying in a straight line directly under his opponent or when the attacker on bottom is lying sideways at an angle under his opponent. Both directional applications are effective, and it's pretty much a matter of preference and opportunity that dictate which is used. However, athletes who have long legs as well as exceptional flexibility tend to favor the straight-on direction when applying a triangle choke, but this isn't a hard-and-fast rule. The photos that follow show these two basic directions.

Basic Straight-On Position from Bottom Guard

The attacker on bottom lies directly in front of his opponent as shown in this photo. This is often considered the standard application of the triangle choke from the bottom guard. A good advantage of this straight-on position is that it allows the attacker on bottom to control his opponent very well with his legs as shown in this photo. The bottom grappler also has the option of spinning and turning to a side angle under his opponent if this initial application doesn't work.

Basic Side Angle Position from Bottom Guard

The attacker on bottom lies at an angle and sideways to his opponent (the two bodies forming somewhat of an "L" shape) as shown in this photo. The advantage of this side angle position is that it allows the bottom grappler to "have longer legs." In other words, the side angle of the bottom grappler's body in relation to the top grappler's position closes the distance between the two grapplers and allows the bottom man to extend his legs further, trapping and forming a triangle easier. This side angle also allows the bottom grappler a good opportunity to roll his opponent over onto his side to complete the strangle or apply an armlock.

THE PRIMARY PARTS OF THE TRIANGLE: ANCHOR LEG AND TIE-UP LEG

Each leg has a specific function when forming a triangle. Fundamentally, the triangle with the legs is formed with (1) an "anchor" leg and (2) a "tie up" leg. The anchor leg is the leg that the attacker slides over his opponent's shoulder and initially uses to trap the defender's head. The tie-up leg is used to form the triangle by hooking onto the anchor leg.

Think of it this way: both legs trap an opponent's head, shoulder, and arm, and the leg that the attacker initially slides over his opponent's shoulder to wrap around his neck is the anchor keeping the opponent's head in place. The other leg is the leg that is used to tie up, secure, and form the triangle, trapping the opponent's head, shoulder, and arm to create the strangling action.

The Anchor Leg

The bottom grappler uses his right leg to slide over his opponent's left shoulder and place it on the left side of his neck. This "anchor" is important, as it is the leg that creates the initial trap that controls the top grappler's head, keeping it in place so that the other leg can be used to form and secure the triangle.

The Tie-Up Leg

The bottom grappler's left leg is the tie-up leg and is placed over his right (anchor) leg and ankle to form the triangle and secure it so it is tight and effective. This action ties the two legs together to more firmly secure the triangle. (More on how to form the triangle a bit later.)

CLEARING THE SHOULDER: SLIDING THE ANCHOR LEG OVER OPPONENT'S SHOULDER TO FORM THE TRIANGLE

It's essential for the bottom grappler to quickly slide his anchor leg over his opponent's shoulder to control the top grappler's head and start to form the triangle with the legs. Sometimes, doing this is a problem, but it's a problem that can be solved with some practice on the mat.

Presented here are some primary methods that the bottom grappler can use to slide his leg over his opponent's shoulder (what I call "clearing the shoulder") and start to form the triangle. Certainly not all the methods of sliding the anchor leg over an opponent's shoulder are presented, but the methods shown all have a good ratio of success. The best thing to do is to experiment during practice to develop a variety of methods to slide the anchor leg over an opponent's shoulder and find the ways that work best for you.

Clear Shoulder: Hand or Lower-Arm Push

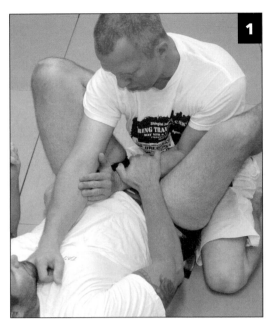

Probably the most fundamental and commonly used way to clear an opponent's shoulder is for the bottom grappler to (as in this photo) use his right hand to grab the top grappler's left hand or forearm.

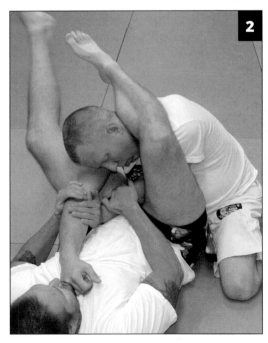

The bottom grappler uses his right hand and arm to shove the top grappler's left hand and arm in and close to the defender's body as shown in this photo. As he does this, the bottom grappler quickly slides his right foot and leg up and over the top grappler's left arm and shoulder.

TECHNICAL TIP: When the attacker clears his opponent's shoulder with his leg, he should slam and hold his leg forcefully against his opponent's neck to ensure a strong start when forming the triangle.

Clear Shoulder: Elbow or Upper Arm Push

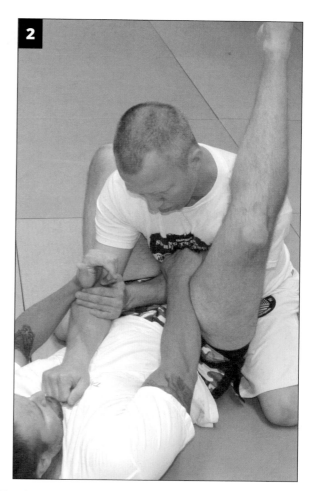

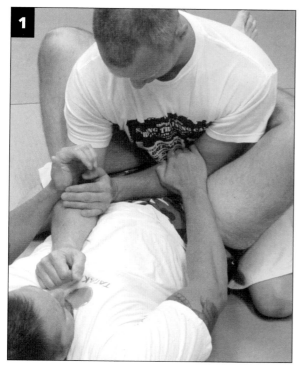

The bottom grappler uses his left hand and arm to shove his opponent's left elbow and arm in close to the top grappler's chest. As he does this, the bottom grappler quickly slides his right foot and leg up and over the top man's left arm and shoulder.

Another common method of clearing the shoulder is for the bottom grappler to use his right hand to grab the top grappler's left elbow or upper arm as shown in this photo.

Clear Shoulder: Opponent Under-hooks with Arm

In many cases, the top grappler will use his left hand and arm (as in this photo) to hook under the bottom grappler's right leg in an attempt to pass his guard.

This can create the opportunity for the bottom grappler to quickly slide his right foot and leg up and over the top grappler's left arm and shoulder to clear the shoulder and set up the triangle.

Clear Shoulder: Trap Opponent's Arm with Knee or Leg

The bottom grappler rolls to his left hip and uses his bent right knee to jam into the top grappler's left arm and trapping it (or at least controlling it) momentarily.

As he does this, the bottom grappler quickly slides his right foot and leg up and over the top grappler's left arm and shoulder as shown in this photo.

Clear Shoulder: Pop Hand Out

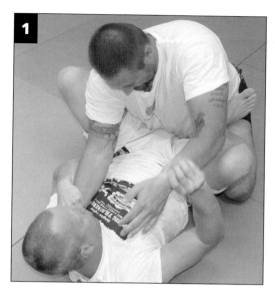

Sometimes, the bottom grappler may use his right hand (as in this photo) to grab the top grappler's left wrist or arm and pull it out and away in a quick motion. In this photo, the bottom man has his right foot placed on the left hip of his opponent and will use it to clear the top man's left shoulder.

The bottom grappler continues to use his right hand to pull the top grappler's left hand out and away from his body. Doing this gives the bottom grappler room to slide his right foot and leg up and over the top grappler's shoulder.

This photo shows how the bottom grappler slides his right foot and leg over his opponent's left arm and shoulder to start to form the triangle.

Clear Shoulder: Knee Wedge and Push

The bottom grappler uses his left knee and shin to jam on the inside of the top grappler's right shoulder and chest area. Doing this creates some space between the two bodies and gives the bottom grappler room to work. As he does this, the bottom grappler uses his left hand to grab his opponent's right elbow as shown.

The bottom grappler quickly uses his left hand to shove the top grappler's right arm back as shown. Doing this gives the bottom grappler some room to move his left foot and leg up and over the top man's right arm and shoulder.

The bottom grappler moves his left leg up and clears his opponent's right arm and shoulder.

Clear Shoulder: Foot on Arm or at Opponent's Elbow

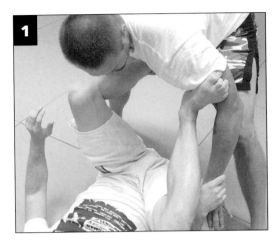

Who says the bottom grappler has to start out with his feet placed on the top grappler's hips or legs? Fighting off of the bottom in the guard position and placing the feet on an opponent's upper body or upper body limbs is an effective way of controlling him. In this photo, the bottom grappler places his right foot on his opponent's left biceps area as the bottom grappler uses his left hand to grab and control the top man's left wrist.

The bottom grappler quickly slides his right foot and leg over the top grappler's left shoulder to start forming the triangle.

Clear Shoulder: Foot on Opponent's Chest or Upper Body

The bottom grappler is fighting his opponent from the bottom guard and uses his right foot to push on the top grappler's left chest or shoulder area.

The bottom grappler may be able to slide his right foot and leg up and over the top grappler's left chest or shoulder area to clear it.

TECHNICAL TIP: There are other methods of clearing the shoulder, but you get the idea. Experiment with this aspect of setting up the triangle in your workouts, but above all make sure to clear the opponent's shoulder as the first step in forming an effective triangle.

After establishing a position to work from, the attacker's first major step in the actual movement of trapping his opponent with the triangle is clearing his opponent's upper arm and shoulder and positioning his anchor leg onto the opponent's shoulder at the neck area. Once this has been done, it's now time to actually form the triangle with the legs and tighten the position so that the choke or strangle is applied in a swift and controlled manner.

TRAPPING THE OPPONENT'S HEAD AND FORMING THE TRIANGLE FROM THE BOTTOM GUARD POSITION

After clearing his opponent's shoulder with his anchor leg, the attacker's (the bottom grappler's) immediate goal is to trap and isolate his opponent's head, shoulder, and arm and (as a result) control as much of the opponent's upper body as possible so the attacker can form a triangle with his legs and squeeze them together to secure the strangle. The bottom grappler (the attacker) must break the top grappler's posture and bend him forward so the bottom grappler can form a tight triangle. To do this, the attacker must control his opponent's head and pull the opponent close so that the bottom grappler can use his legs to greater effect. It's also important for the attacker to be as precise as he can with his leg placement and positioning to get the quickest and most effective strangle possible with the triangle.

Let's continue to examine the anchor leg's job before looking at how the tie-up leg comes into play to secure the triangle.

Anchor Leg on Side of Opponent's Neck

Attacker Traps Opponent's Head with His Anchor Leg

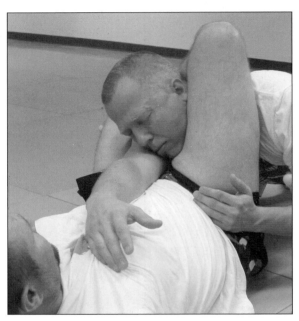

This photo shows the bottom grappler's right inner thigh placed directly and securely on the left side of the top grappler's neck where his carotid artery is. The carotid arteries run on each side of the neck, and jamming the inner thigh securely against it starts the strangling process. Much like a snake wraps around its victim, continually squeezing to cut the blood off from the brain, the attacker's leg traps his opponent's neck to start the squeezing process of the strangle.

TECHNICAL TIP: The bottom grappler drives his hips in as close as possible to the top grappler's upper body as shown in this photo.

The bottom grappler positions his right leg (the leg that slid over the top grappler's left shoulder) and bends his leg so that the top grappler's head is trapped between the upper leg and the lower leg as shown in this photo.

TECHNICAL TIP: The attacker's right ankle and foot are positioned lower than his knee so that the attacker (the bottom grappler) has more control of the top grappler's head. Think of it this way: the defender's head is a nut and the attacker's anchor leg (right leg in these photos) is the nutcracker trapping and tightening the nut wedged in it.

After Trapping the Opponent's Head, the Attacker Controls the Opponent's Head with His Anchor Leg

Control Opponent's Arm to Cinch the Triangle in Tighter Around the Neck, Shoulder, Arm, and Head

The bottom grappler uses his right leg to trap the top grappler's head. As he does this, the bottom grappler uses the strength of his leg to pull the top grappler's head forward and down so that the bottom grappler can more easily use his left leg to form the triangle. This position may not be held for very long, but the effect of it results in the bottom grappler (the attacker) trapping and controlling the top grappler's head long enough to quickly use the other leg as the tie-up leg to form the triangle.

As the attacker gains control over his opponent's head, he can also use one or both hands to pull or manipulate his opponent's arm to better position himself to form and tighten the triangle. This photo shows the attacker pulling his opponent's arm across his body into position. While this is an important step, it's also important to not make a "big deal" about it. Doing so will trigger the opponent's reaction of pulling away too early and possibly stopping the entire process.

USING THE HANDS TO CINCH IN THE ANCHOR LEG AND CONTROL THE OPPONENT'S HEAD

In some cases, it's a real advantage for the bottom grappler to use one or both of his hands to grab his foot, ankle, or leg (or grab his opponent's head, neck, or other body part) to help control his opponent's head in order to manipulate his foot into position behind the knee of his other leg (the tie-up leg) to form a triangle.

Often, by using his hands to grab his ankle, foot, or leg, the attacker can better manipulate his legs into a stronger triangle. The attacker's main goal is to form a triangle with his legs. How he does that is limited by the rules of the sport, but more often it is only limited by the grappler's imagination and range of skill.

The next four photos show a basic (yet effective) method of manipulating the foot and leg into place behind the other leg's knee to form a firm triangle.

Attacker Grabs His Anchor Leg to Use as a Handle to Break the Defender's Posture and Pull His Head Down

The top grappler's head is still somewhat upright even though the bottom grappler has used his left leg to clear the top man's right shoulder. To effectively break the upright posture of the top grappler, the bottom grappler must pull the top man's head down. Using his anchor leg (the left leg in this photo) as a lever, the bottom grappler can better pull his opponent's head down low enough to form the triangle.

The bottom grappler uses his left leg (with the left lower leg wedged directly behind the top grappler's neck and head) to pull the head down. Look at how the bottom grappler uses his right hand to grab his left ankle to assist in pulling the opponent's head lower. At this point, the bottom grappler has succeeded in breaking the top grappler's posture by pulling his head down low enough to start to form the triangle.

By using his left leg as the anchor to bend his opponent over and drive his head down, the bottom grappler continues to use his right hand to hold onto his left ankle as he swings his right leg (the tie-up leg) over his left foot and ankle to start to form the triangle.

After making sure that his left ankle and foot are placed firmly in the back of his knee, the bottom grappler drives his right leg down to tie in the triangle firmly.

TECHNICAL TIP: When the attacker wants to control his opponent's head or posture or tighten his triangle, the ideal situation is for him to grab his ankle or lower leg rather than grab his lower foot or toes. The attacker has more control of his entire leg when he grabs his ankle (at or above the joint) or lower leg (at the shin) to help place his foot on the inside of his knee to form the triangle or pull his opponent's head down. However, sometimes circumstances may only permit the attacker to grab his lower foot or toes to secure the triangle and do what is necessary to get the job done. It may not be perfect, but if it gets the job done, that's what counts.

The attacker has better control of his foot and leg if he grabs his ankle (above the joint) or lower leg as shown here. The lower leg doesn't bend, and grabbing low on the leg allows the attacker to more freely manipulate his leg to control his opponent.

Sometimes, the attacker may have to grab his toes or the top of his foot as shown here. This isn't an ideal situation because grabbing anywhere on the foot below the ankle joint will cause the foot to bend. But then maybe there are some situations where the attacker may want to bend his foot a specific way so he can place it in the back of his other knee to form the triangle.

This photo shows how the attacker uses his left hand to grab the toes of his right foot to manipulate his right foot in place behind his left knee and cinch in the triangle. This may not always be the strongest way of moving a foot in place, but as said before, the situation may dictate doing what is necessary to get the job done.

USING THE TIE-UP LEG TO SECURE, TIGHTEN, AND FORM THE TRIANGLE

The anchor leg has done its job; it has initially trapped and isolated the opponent's head, and as result has also controlled his upper body. Now, the attacker will use his tie-up leg to literally tie up his opponent and form the triangle.

Feeding the Foot into the Knee: The Attacker Places His Foot inside His Knee to Form the Triangle

IMPORTANT: Be precise when placing the foot in the back of the knee.

This photo shows the attacker using his right hand to grab his right lower leg or ankle (the anchor leg) to place it in the back of his left knee (the tie-up leg).

The attacker places his right ankle and foot on the inside of his left knee joint to start to form the triangle. It is important that the attacker be careful and precise in placing his right foot or ankle in his left knee. The attacker has some time (not much) to do this as he is controlling the position, and he must make sure that the triangle is formed firmly.

TECHNICAL TIP: The attacker must make sure to place his foot or ankle precisely and firmly in the back of his other knee to securely form the triangle. The attacker must be efficient in his movement and waste no time or movement. As is often said, "Take your time, but do it in a hurry!" In other words, be precise, be quick, and get the foot in the back of the knee to get a tight, secure triangle.

THE ATTACKER'S FOOT POSITION IS ESSENTIAL TO A TIGHT TRIANGLE

The following three photos illustrate the importance of the position of the foot placement of the anchor leg in the back of the knee of the tie-up leg. The first two photos show the correct way of placing the anchor foot in the back of the knee and the third photo shows a weaker (and often less effective) way of placing the anchor foot in the back of the tie-up leg.

Attacker's Toe Is Pointed up with His Ankle Hooked in the Back of His Knee

This photo shows how the bottom grappler's right leg is placed over his left ankle to form the triangle. The bottom grappler's left foot is pointed so that his toes are

pointed upward and his left foot is firmly placed in the back of his right bent knee. The bottom grappler further tightens the triangle by driving his right foot downward and pointing his toe for added power. It is important to place the top of the foot or ankle inside the knee as shown for the tightest control possible when forming the triangle. Remember: toes up and heel down for a secure triangle.

Attacker's Foot Firmly Placed in the Back of the Knee

This photo shows how the attacker's right foot is jammed securely in the back of his left bent knee. The top of the bottom grappler's right foot is firmly placed in the back of his left knee in this photo. Doing this ensures the ankle is firmly locked in place at the back of the knee as well, forming a strong triangle.

A Common Mistake: The Attacker's Foot Is not Placed Deeply Enough Behind His Knee

This photo shows how the attacker's left foot hasn't been placed deeply enough behind his right knee. This results in a weaker triangle because the attacker's left foot will tend to bend (since it's a joint and will bend to its natural range of motion). With this bending of the joint, the triangle may not be as strong as necessary to secure the opponent's head and get the tap out.

Trap Opponent's Head, Shoulder, and Arm with Triangle

At this point, the attacker makes sure to trap his opponent's head (and neck), shoulder, and arm in the triangle. While there are some triangles that trap only the opponent's

head, the most common (and often effective) method is to trap the opponent's head, shoulder, and arm.

TECHNICAL TIP: In this photo, the attacker's right thigh is jammed in the left side of the top grappler's neck. The top grappler's head, right shoulder, and arm are trapped with the attacker's left leg (the tie-up leg). The pressure applied from the right leg squeezing the left side of the neck, the pressure from the right shoulder and arm trapped in the right side of the defender's neck, and the downward pressure placed on the defender's head from the attacker's right (anchor) leg create the necessary pressure to cause the strangling action.

SOME USEFUL METHODS FOR HOW THE ATTACKER CAN USE HIS HANDS TO CONTROL THE OPPONENT'S HEAD TO FORM THE TRIANGLE

Use Both Hands to Pull Opponent's Head

The bottom grappler uses both of his hands to pull his opponent's head downward. Doing this allows the bottom grappler to more effectively hook his right leg (his anchor leg) over his opponent's head and neck.

TECHNICAL TIP: The attacker should use his hand or hands to pull down on the top grappler's head to better hook the anchor leg and prevent the top grappler from "posturing up" or sitting upright (that could prevent the triangle from being formed).

The bottom grappler pulls his opponent's head down enough so that he can hook his legs together to form the triangle.

Attacker Uses One Hand to Pull Opponent's Head and One Hand to Pull His Leg

The bottom grappler uses his right hand to cup the back of his opponent's head to pull it down. As he does this, the attacker uses his left hand to grab his right lower leg to place it under his knee to form the triangle.

The bottom grappler uses the side of his fist and lower arm to hook behind his opponent's head in order to pull it down low enough to form the triangle with his legs.

TECHNICAL TIP: The attacker should use his hands in any way possible to manipulate and control his opponent. The hands, arms, feet, and leg each have specific (but related) tasks in forming the triangle.

Attacker Uses Both Hands to Pull His Leg and Form the Triangle

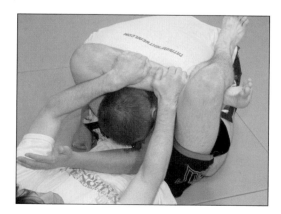

A common (and effective) way to pull the anchor leg and control the opponent's head is for the attacker to use both hands to grab his lower leg and pull downward.

Attacker Uses the Same-Side Hand and Leg

Sometimes, the attacker may use his right hand to grab his right leg to pull down onto his opponent's head as shown in this photo. It usually doesn't matter which hand the attacker uses, just as long as he gets the job done.

Attacker Uses One Hand to Pull Opponent's Arm as He Uses the Other Hand to Grab His Leg or Ankle

The bottom grappler uses his right hand and arm to trap his opponent's right arm. As he does this, the bottom grappler uses his left hand to grab his right leg and move it into place to secure a tighter triangle.

A Necktie: The Attacker Uses His Arm to Grab His Leg and Choke His Opponent

Sometimes the attacker can use his arm to not only grab and manipulate his leg or foot, but can use it to choke his opponent as shown here. There will be more on "neckties" later.

Body Triangle: Control and Apply Pressure

The bottom grappler forms a triangle around his opponent's torso so that the triangle is formed slightly under the top grappler's ribs and above his hips directly around his stomach. Doing this creates a strong hold that the bottom grappler can use to exert a great deal of pressure to force the top man to submit. Even if there isn't sufficient pressure for the top grappler to tap out, the bottom grappler can use this body triangle to control his opponent so he can apply another choke such as this kata jime (shoulder choke—also called an arm triangle choke) as shown in this photo.

"Head Only" Triangle Choke

When using a "head only" triangle choke, the bottom grappler does not trap his opponent's arm or shoulder but instead traps only his opponent's head with his legs. In many cases, as shown in this photo, the attacker will use a hand or arm to wedge his opponent's neck to add more pressure to the carotid artery. The rules of many combat sports stipulate that the head and arm must be trapped inside the triangle, but in some fighting sports or in a fight, trapping only the head is a viable and nasty way to perform a triangle choke.

TRIANGLE CHOKES FROM THE BOTTOM GUARD POSITION

Okay, up to now, this part of the book has examined the core skills of a triangle choke from the bottom guard position. The basics are essential, and after gaining both skill and confidence in them, it's time to work into the practical applications of doing a triangle choke from the bottom guard. Sure enough, not every possible triangle choke variation or application is presented on these pages, but quite a few are and it's hoped that these techniques impel you to adapt what you see and make it work for you.

#1 Core Triangle Application from Straight on When in Bottom Guard

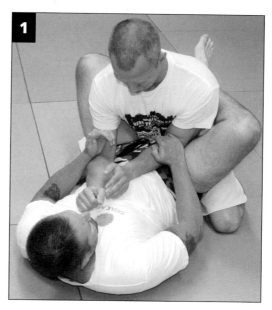

The bottom grappler has his opponent in his guard and is using his right hand to trap his opponent's left forearm as shown.

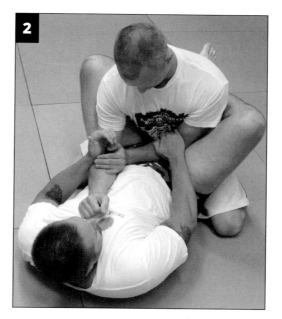

The bottom grappler uses his right hand to shove his opponent's left forearm and elbow back and into the top grappler's torso as shown.

As the bottom grappler continues to use his right hand to shove his opponent's left arm and elbow into the top grappler's torso, the bottom man starts to move his right leg up and over the top man's left arm and shoulder.

The bottom grappler slides his right leg up and over the top grappler's left shoulder as the bottom man continues to use his right hand and arm to shove his opponent's left arm into the top man's torso.

The bottom grappler makes it a point to slam his right leg hard and tight against the left side of the top grappler's neck. As he does this, the bottom grappler moves his right hand and arm so that he now uses his right hand to push and control the top grappler's left hip. Doing this isolates the top grappler's hip and controls his movement temporarily. The bottom grappler drives his right foot downward and across the back of his opponent's neck. Doing this pulls the top grappler's head down, making it easier for the bottom grappler to control the top man's body (and prevent the top grappler from posturing upright). It also makes it easier for the bottom grappler to start to form a strong triangle with his right (anchor) leg and his tie-up (left) leg.

At this point, the bottom grappler uses both of his hands to grab the top grappler's right arm and pull it. Doing this pulls the top grappler in tighter to the bottom man's torso. This action allows the bottom grappler to drive his right (anchor) leg tighter around the top grappler's head and neck as shown. As he does this, the bottom grappler moves his left leg up and is preparing to form a triangle.

The bottom grappler forms a triangle with his feet and legs as shown. As he does this, the bottom grappler pulls with both hands on his opponent's right arm. This pulls the top grappler in tight and allows the bottom grappler to form a tighter triangle with his legs.

The bottom grappler applies pressure with his legs as he arches with his hips and uses both hands to pull the top grappler in tight to secure the choke and get the tap out.

TECHNICAL TIP: This application of the triangle choke may be basic, but don't let "basic" fool you. This is a popular and effective choke and one that world-class fighters use time and time again with great success. When it comes down to it, world-class skills are simply fundamentals performed to their full potential.

#2 Core Triangle Application from Side Angle When in Bottom Guard Position

This is a strong position to secure the triangle choke and allows the bottom grappler to "lengthen" his legs and makes the triangle possible for grapplers who may have short legs.

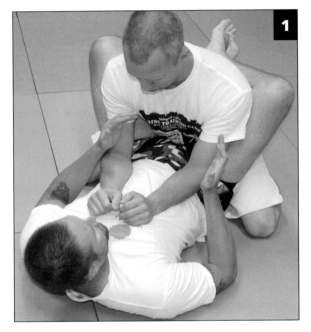

The bottom grappler has his opponent in his guard as shown.

The bottom grappler uses his right hand to shove his opponent's left forearm into the top grappler's torso as shown. As he does this, the bottom grappler starts to move his right leg up and onto his opponent's left upper arm.

The bottom grappler uses his right leg to clear his opponent's left shoulder as shown. As he does this, the bottom grappler uses his right hand to grab (palm up) on the inside of the top grappler's left upper leg and thigh. The bottom grappler uses his right hand that is grabbing his opponent's left leg to pull his upper body closer to the top man's left knee.

The bottom grappler uses his left hand and arm to pull himself so that his head is close to his opponent's left knee as shown. Look at the side angle that the bottom grappler has in this photo. The bottom grappler also forms the triangle with his legs and uses his left hand to pull the top grappler's right arm in tight, allowing the bottom grappler to form a tight triangle with his legs as shown.

The bottom grappler can squeeze his opponent's neck with his legs from this position and get the tap out. But, in some cases, the bottom grappler may be able to start to roll his opponent over and onto his back.

The bottom grappler uses his left hand to grab and hook his opponent's left leg as shown as the bottom grappler rolls the top grappler over onto his side.

The bottom grappler rolls his opponent over and applies both a triangle choke with his legs and a juji gatame (cross-body armlock). This finish position is what is known as "double trouble" because the attacker is using both a triangle choke and an armlock, making it double trouble for his opponent.

TECHNICAL TIP: A WORD OR TWO ON "DOUBLE TROUBLE"

In many situations, the attacker secures both a triangle choke and an armlock; or a triangle choke and a hold-down; or a triangle choke and a leglock. In other words, the attacker is choking his opponent with a triangle choke and applying some other type of submission or finishing hold as well. This is what is called "double trouble." And, in some cases, it can even be triple trouble if the attacker has a triangle choke and combines it with two other finishing holds or techniques. So, whenever possible, try to get an opponent into double trouble. If he doesn't tap out from the choke, he'll tap out from the armlock (or other finishing hold)!

#3 Use Triangle Choke When Top Grappler Posts on One Knee to Pass Guard

This is a common situation where the top grappler comes up on one knee (in this series of photos, the left knee) in an attempt to either pass the bottom grappler's guard or post and stabilize the bottom grappler's leg and foot in order to do a leg or ankle lock. In some cases, a novice grappler or fighter will come up on one knee in an attempt to either stabilize his position or attempt to stand. This photo shows the top grappler using his left arm to grab the bottom grappler's leg before he comes up on a knee.

The top grappler steps up on his left foot. The bottom grappler immediately uses his right hand and arm to hook and grab the top grappler's left lower leg or grab under the left knee as shown. As he does this, the bottom grappler pulls his body to his right with his lead arm close to the top grappler's left bent knee.

The bottom grappler forms a triangle with his legs as shown and uses his right hand and arm to hook and lift his opponent's left knee. As he does this, the bottom grappler uses his left hand and arm to pull on his opponent's right arm. Doing this forces the top grappler to roll over to his right side as shown.

The bottom grappler finishes the move by squeezing his legs to get the triangle choke as he arches his hips and pulls with both hands on his opponent's right arm to secure the armlock.

#4 Foot on Knee and Push to Secure Triangle from Bottom Guard

Collapsing the top grappler by pushing on one or both of his knees is a common and effective way to control his body. This photo shows the bottom grappler positioning his right foot on his opponent's left knee.

This photo shows the bottom grappler's right foot placement on his opponent's left knee to start the attack.

The bottom grappler uses his right foot and leg to push against his opponent's left knee. Doing this will either push the top grappler's left knee back or may even push the bottom grappler back and away from his opponent. Either way, the bottom grappler is creating distance between his body and his opponent's body as shown. The bottom grappler uses his left hand and arm to pull on his opponent's right arm, stretching it. The bottom grappler also uses his right hand to push the top grappler's left arm back so the bottom man will be able to use his right leg to clear his opponent's left arm and shoulder.

The bottom grappler uses his right leg to move up and over the top grappler's left arm and shoulder as shown. As he does this, the bottom grappler uses both hands to pull on his opponent's right arm so the bottom man can tighten the triangle he is forming with his legs.

This photo shows the bottom grappler using his right leg (his anchor leg) to trap his opponent's head and neck. The bottom grappler is moving his left leg up and is about to form the triangle. As he does this, the bottom grappler uses both hands to pull on his opponent's right arm, pulling the top man in tight and creating the space necessary to form the triangle with his legs.

The bottom grappler forms the triangle with his legs.

This side view shows the bottom grappler using his feet and legs to tighten the triangle. The top grappler may submit from either the choke or the armlock at this point.

If the bottom grappler deems it necessary, he can roll to his left side, forcing his opponent to fall onto his right side as shown in this photo. The bottom grappler can apply a strong triangle choke and a strong armlock from this finish position.

#5 Double Knee Push and Flatten Opponent

The bottom grappler starts the move with both of her feet placed on the top grappler's knees as shown.

The bottom grappler pushes with both of her feet onto the top grappler's knees, forcing him to collapse on his front as shown.

The bottom grappler immediately rolls onto her right side as she swings her left foot and leg over her opponent's head.

As she does this, the bottom grappler uses both of her hands and arms to trap and pull on her opponent's right arm.

The bottom grappler forms a triangle by placing the top of her left foot on the inside of her right knee as shown. The bottom grappler is laying on her right side as shown as she uses both hands and arms to pull on her opponent's right arm. Doing this creates both a triangle choke and an armlock to get the tap out.

#6 Knee Slide Over Shoulder to Triangle from Bottom Guard

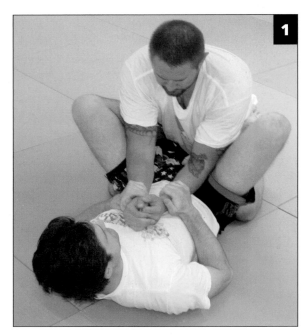

The bottom grappler has both of his feet wedged in the top grappler's hips to start this move.

The bottom grappler rolls to his left as he moves his right bent knee up and onto his opponent's left arm as shown.

The bottom grappler slides his right bent knee up his opponent's left arm and shoulder.

The bottom grappler moves his right leg up and over the top grappler's left arm and shoulder and positions his right leg at the left side of the top grappler's neck and head. Notice that the bottom grappler uses his left hand and arm to trap the top grappler's extended right arm to the bottom man's body.

The bottom grappler forms the triangle with his legs and applies pressure to get the submission.

#7 Attacker Pushes with His Feet on His Opponent's Hips

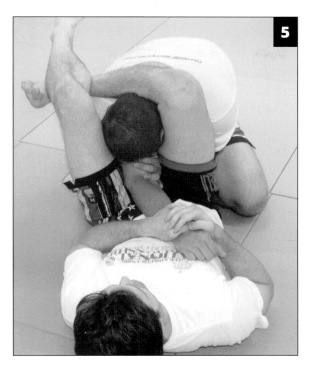

This is a common (and effective) way for the bottom grappler to control the space between his body and the top grappler's body. In this situation, the bottom grappler has both of his feet wedged in the hips of the top grappler.

The bottom grappler pushes with both of his feet and legs against the top grappler's hips, which creates space between the two fighters. As he does this, the bottom grappler uses his left hand to grab and trap the top grappler's right arm, extending it as shown. The bottom grappler wants to make space between his body and his opponent's body so he has the space he needs to form a triangle with his legs.

The bottom grappler quickly moves his body to his right as he swings his right leg up and over the top grappler's left arm and shoulder as shown.

The bottom grappler forms a triangle with his legs as shown.

The bottom grappler finishes the move by rolling to his left as he uses both hands to pull on his opponent's extended right arm. Doing this traps the opponent in a triangle choke and a juji gatame (cross-body armlock).

#8 Attacker Hugs Opponent's Head to Distract Him and Control His Head

The bottom grappler has a closed guard by hooking his feet together around his opponent as shown. As he does this, the bottom grappler uses both of his hands and arms to trap and pull the top grappler's head down and hug it to his chest.

The bottom grappler maintains control of his opponent's head as shown. As he does this, the bottom grappler starts to move his feet and legs to begin his triangle.

The bottom grappler uses his right hand to grab and shove his opponent's left upper arm back as shown. Doing this allows the bottom man the room he needs to start to move his right leg up and over his opponent's left arm and shoulder.

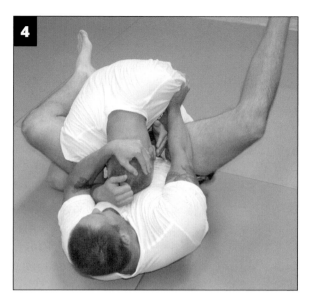

The bottom grappler moves his right leg up as he continues to use his right hand to shove his opponent's left arm back.

TECHNICAL TIP: Trapping the top grappler's head allows the bottom grappler a better opportunity to slide his right leg behind it. This prevents the top grappler from "posturing up." If the top grappler is able to posture up, he can prevent the bottom grappler from forming a good triangle.

The bottom grappler moves his right foot and leg up and over his opponent's left arm and shoulder. As he

continues to use his right hand to trap the top grappler's head down, the bottom grappler uses his right hand to grab and help position his right leg up and behind the top man's head.

The bottom grappler moves his left (tie-up) leg up and into position so he can position his right (anchor) leg and form a triangle. The bottom grappler continues to use his left hand to trap the top grappler's head down on the bottom man's chest.

The bottom grappler has successfully formed a triangle with his feet and legs. He uses his left hand to continue to pull down on the top grappler's head as he uses his right hand to trap the top grappler's right arm to the bottom man's torso. The bottom grappler will arch his hips as he applies pressure with his legs to secure the triangle choke.

#9 The Russian Drag to the Triangle Choke (In Actual Competition)

This sequence of photos taken at the National AAU Freestyle Judo Championships shows Derrick Darling using the Russian drag setup to choke his opponent with the triangle choke. The attacker started his triangle choke from the bottom guard. The defender (on the right in the photo) stepped up with his left knee in an attempt to escape the triangle and pass the bottom grappler's guard.

The bottom grappler uses his right hand to grab under his opponent's left knee as shown in this photo. As he does this, the bottom grappler spins his body to his right, getting closer to his opponent's left knee. Doing this closes the space between the bottom grappler and his opponent.

The bottom grappler grabs his hands together, and as he does this, he pulls the top grappler's left leg toward him, pulling the leg straight as shown. The bottom grappler grasps his opponent's left leg tightly to his torso. This results in the top grappler falling on his left leg and hip as shown. This action of collapsing an opponent in this way is what is called the "Russian drag."

With the top grappler compromised, the bottom grappler tightens the triangle choke as he collapses the defender onto his buttocks in a seated position and gets the tap out.

#10 The Russian Drag to the Triangle Choke (an Analysis)

The move starts with the bottom grappler in an open guard and the top grappler on his knees as shown.

As he starts to form a triangle with his legs around the top grappler's head and shoulder, the bottom grappler uses his right hand and arm to pull the top grappler's left leg. The bottom grappler pulls the top man's left leg so that the top grappler collapses back and onto his buttocks.

As the top grappler steps up on his left foot (as shown), the bottom grappler slides his right foot and leg up and over the top man's left arm and shoulder and moves his body to his right and close to the top grappler's left foot. As he does this, the bottom grappler uses his right hand to reach under and around the top grappler's left foot and ankle as shown.

The bottom grappler uses his left hand and arm to grab and trap the top grappler's extended right arm as shown. The bottom grappler has formed a secure triangle with his legs and uses his right hand and arm to trap and pull the top grappler's extended left foot and leg as shown. The top grappler's position is compromised and he is trapped sitting on his buttocks. The bottom grappler may be able to finish the move at this point with both a triangle choke and an armlock.

The bottom grappler may finish the move by rolling to his right as shown. Doing this creates additional pressure to both the choke and the armlock.

TECHNICAL TIP #1 ON THE RUSSIAN DRAG: Sometimes, the Russian drag will knock the defender back onto his buttocks and the attacker may not be able to roll the defender over onto his side. If that's the case, the attacker can secure the triangle choke from this seated position.

TECHNICAL TIP #2 ON THE RUSSIAN DRAG: A triangle choke can work from just about any position as shown in this photo and the previous series of photos where the attacker has taken the defender onto his buttocks in a seated (and compromised) position. In some situations, a well-done Russian drag is the reason the defender has been broken down into a seated position as shown here.

#11 Top Grappler Stands Up to Escape but Bottom Grappler Secures the Triangle Choke

A good defense for the top grappler against the triangle choke is to stand up and get onto his foot before the bottom grappler can effectively form a triangle with his feet and legs. This photo shows the bottom grappler forming a triangle and the top grappler about to stand. As he senses the top man is about to stand, the bottom grappler uses his right hand and arm to reach under the top grappler's body as shown. The bottom grappler also uses his left hand and arm to trap the top grappler's right arm.

As the top grappler starts to stand (in this photo, the top grappler steps up and onto his left foot). The bottom grappler immediately uses his right hand and arm to reach under the top grappler's left lower leg. As he does this, the bottom grappler moves his body to his right so that his head is close to the top grappler's left foot. Look at the side angle that the bottom grappler has now created.

As the top grappler continues to stand, the bottom grappler uses his right hand to grab and hook the top grappler's left foot and ankle as shown. Look at how the bottom grappler has moved his head as close as possible to the top man's left foot. This spinning action taken by the bottom grappler is crucial to preventing the top grappler from standing and stopping the triangle choke.

This photo shows how the bottom grappler moves his body under his opponent as he uses his right leg to drive the top grappler's head down toward the mat. The bottom grappler must control the top grappler's head and drive it down, preventing the top man from standing upright.

The bottom grappler continues to spin to his right as he forms a triangle with his feet and legs. Look at how the bottom grappler uses his left hand and arm to trap the top man's extended right arm. Look at how the bottom grappler uses his right hand and arm to hook and grab the top grappler's left leg.

The combination of the spinning action along with the control of the top grappler's extended right arm and his left leg allows the bottom grappler to roll and collapse the top man over as shown.

As he rolls the top grappler over, the bottom grappler secures the triangle choke and the armlock.

#12 Attacker Is Fighting an Opponent Who Is Standing

The bottom grappler is fighting an opponent who is standing.

The bottom grappler's initial task is to get as close as possible and under his opponent as shown in this photo. The bottom grappler uses his left hand to grab his opponent's right forearm and his right hand to grab and control his opponent's left forearm. As he does this, the bottom grappler forcefully moves his left foot and leg up and over his opponent's right shoulder.

The bottom grappler drives his hips up and toward his opponent, and the bottom grappler continues to form the triangle with his feet and legs.

The bottom grappler may have to raise his hips and buttocks off of the mat as shown as he quickly moves his left leg (the anchor leg) over his opponent's head and neck as shown. The bottom grappler uses his right leg to start to form the triangle.

As he forms his triangle with his feet and legs, the bottom grappler uses his right hand to pull the top grappler's left arm across the bottom man's body as shown. Doing this helps tighten the triangle.

The bottom grappler has a strong triangle formed with his legs and continues to pull with both hands on his opponent's arms so that the bottom grappler rolls to his right and to the top grappler's left as shown.

Doing this collapses the top grappler onto his left side as the bottom grappler applies both the triangle choke and the armlock for double trouble from this position.

#13 Triangle Choke When Opponent Stands

If the top grappler manages to stand up, the bottom grappler still can secure a strong triangle choke from this position.

The bottom grappler has his opponent in his guard and is actively working to secure a triangle choke from this position.

The bottom grappler forms his triangle choke as shown. The top grappler senses he is in trouble and starts to stand.

3

The bottom grappler quickly uses his right hand and arm to grab and hook on the inside of the top grappler's left leg as shown. The bottom grappler should do this first to "lace" and control the top grappler's leg and control his movement. The bottom grappler spins to his right so that his head is close to the top grappler's left leg and foot. All the while, the bottom grappler continues to cinch in the triangle with his legs as shown.

4

The bottom grappler uses his right hand to grab and control the top grappler's left lower leg as shown. As he does this, the bottom grappler continues to move his

head to his right and close to the top grappler's left foot and leg. Doing this closes the space between the bottom grappler and the top grappler and tightens the triangle that the bottom grappler has formed.

5

The bottom grappler applies the triangle choke even when the top grappler stands.

TECHNICAL TIP: The most important thing for the bottom grappler to do is to prevent the top grappler from standing upright. It is imperative that the bottom grappler use his anchor leg (in this photo, his right leg) placed across the back of the top grappler's head and neck and apply downward pressure to prevent the top grappler from standing upright. Keeping the top grappler bent over allows the bottom grappler the opportunity to apply the triangle choke from this position.

#14 Attacker Starts with a Foot on His Opponent's Upper Arm or Shoulder

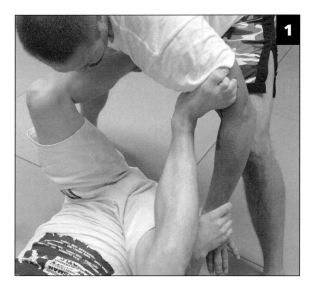

Sometimes, the bottom grappler uses his foot or feet to push against the top grappler's arms or shoulders. This is a fairly common form of using the feet when fighting from the bottom guard position.

The bottom grappler slides his right foot and leg up and over his opponent's left shoulder to start to form the triangle.

The bottom grappler uses his right foot to push against the top grappler's left shoulder as shown in this photo.

The bottom grappler makes sure to move to his right and drive his hips up and into the top grappler so there is little space between the bottom grappler's right leg and thigh and the top grappler's left shoulder and side of the neck. As he does this, the bottom grappler uses his left hand to pull the top grappler's right arm. Doing this helps the bottom grappler pull the top man in closer.

The bottom grappler has spun to his right as shown as he uses his right leg to hook over the top grappler's neck and head.

The bottom grappler forms the triangle with his feet and legs as shown.

To tighten the hold, the bottom grappler uses his left hand (or both hands if he chooses) to pull the top grappler's right arm across the bottom grappler's torso as shown.

The bottom grappler applies the triangle choke as he applies the armlock to get a tap out from both the strangle and the armlock.

#15 Defender Is Standing with Bottom Grappler Closing the Distance to Apply the Triangle Choke

The bottom grappler is using his right foot to push against the top grappler's left upper arm.

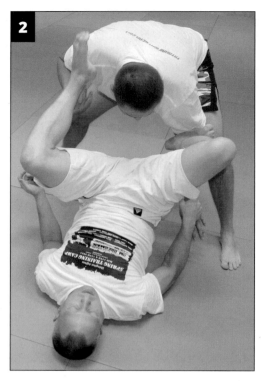

The bottom grappler continues to push with his right foot on his opponent's left upper arm as he quickly moves his left foot and leg up and over the top grappler's right arm and shoulder.

The bottom grappler drives hard so that his hips are off the mat as he drives his left leg across the top grappler's neck and head as shown. The bottom grappler uses his right hand to grab and control the top grappler's left wrist and arm.

The bottom grappler forms the triangle with his feet and legs.

The bottom grappler uses both hands to pull and control the top grappler's left arm as the bottom grappler tightens the triangle choke. As he does this, the bottom grappler uses his legs to force the top grappler to collapse to the mat as shown.

The bottom grappler secures the triangle choke and the armlock to get the tap out.

The bottom grappler uses both of his hands and arms to pull the top grappler's left extended arm across the torso of the bottom grappler. Doing this helps tighten the triangle.

#16 Top Grappler Hooks Under the Bottom Grappler's Leg in an Attempt to Pass Guard

This is a common situation where the top grappler uses one arm to hook the bottom grappler's leg in an attempt to swing it out of the way to pass the bottom grappler's guard.

The top grappler uses his left hand and arm to grab and hook the bottom grappler's right leg as shown.

The bottom grappler quickly drives his right leg up and over the top grappler's left upper arm and shoulder as shown. As he does this, the bottom grappler uses both hands to pull on the top grappler's right arm.

The bottom grappler starts to form a triangle with his feet and legs by moving his left leg up as shown.

The bottom grappler forms the triangle with his feet and legs as he continues to pull on the top grappler's extended right arm.

The bottom grappler tightens the triangle choke as he arches his hips and continues to use both hands to pull on the top grappler's arm. Doing this produces a double trouble situation, and the top grappler taps out from both the choke and the armlock.

#17 Triangle Choke Against Opponent on Top Punching

The top grappler is using his right hand to punch at the bottom grappler.

The bottom fighter uses his left hand and arm to block his opponent's punch.

TECHNICAL TIP: No situation is the same but the bottom fighter's primary concern at this point is to defend himself. The bottom fighter should use any viable way to block, parry, or stop his opponent's punch so that the bottom fighter can survive his opponent's onslaught and go on to escape or counter with an attack of his own; in this case, the bottom fighter will counter with a triangle choke.

The bottom grappler uses his left knee and shin to jam under the top grappler's right armpit. As he does this, the bottom grappler uses his right hand to start to grab behind the top grappler's head. The bottom grappler uses his left hand to grab and control the top grappler's right arm at the elbow.

The bottom grappler uses his left hand to grab the top man's right arm.

The bottom grappler uses his right hand to firmly grab and pull down on the top grappler's head. As he does this, the bottom grappler continues to wedge his left knee against the top grappler's right pectoral area.

The bottom grappler uses his left hand to push the top grappler's right arm back as shown. As he does this, the bottom grappler starts to move his left leg up so that he can swing his left foot and leg over the top grappler's right shoulder. The bottom grappler may have to temporarily let go with his left hand of his opponent's right arm so that he can move his left foot and leg up and over the top grappler's right arm and shoulder.

The bottom grappler uses his left hand to continue to push the top grappler's right arm back as the bottom man moves his left foot and leg up and over the top grappler's right arm and shoulder as shown.

The bottom grappler places his left leg over the right shoulder of the top grappler as the bottom man uses his right hand to help pull his left leg across the top grappler's neck and head, forcing his head down.

The bottom grappler swings or moves his right foot and leg up so that he can form the triangle. At this point, the bottom grappler uses his left hand to grab and pull the top grappler's left arm across the bottom grappler's torso as shown.

The bottom grappler forms the triangle with his feet and legs as tightly as possible. As he does this, the bottom grappler continues to use his left hand to pull on the top grappler's extended left arm.

The bottom grappler has a strong triangle choke and armlock to get the tap out.

#18 Triangle Choke Counter to Can Opener

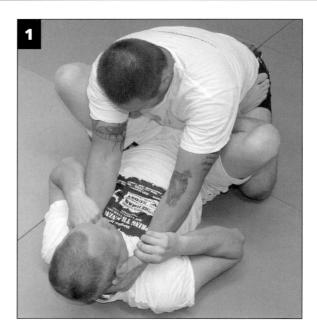

The top grappler is using both of his hands to grab and pull on the bottom grappler's head in an effort to create a neck crank (can opener). The bottom grappler uses both of his hands to grab his opponent's hands as shown.

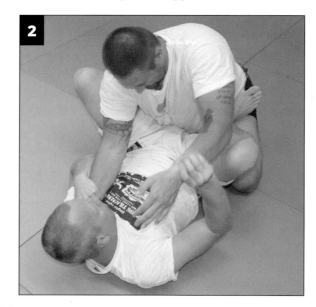

The bottom grappler uses his right hand to peel off the top grappler's left hand as shown. The bottom grappler uses his left hand to grab and trap the top grappler's right hand.

The bottom grappler moves his right foot and leg up and over the top grappler's left shoulder. To make room to do this, the bottom grappler uses his right hand to pull the top grappler's left hand and arm away as shown.

The bottom grappler drives his right foot and leg up and over the top grappler's left shoulder and hooks the top man's head with the right leg as shown.

The bottom grappler uses his left hand to grab his right shin or ankle to help form the triangle as he moves his left foot and leg up.

The bottom grappler forms the triangle with his feet and leg and he continues to use his right hand to grab and push the top grappler's left wrist and arm, keeping it away from the action that is taking place. The bottom grappler applies pressure with his legs and gets the tap out from the triangle choke.

#19 Upside Down Triangle Choke from Bottom Guard

The bottom grappler has his opponent in his guard as shown.

The bottom grappler spins his body to his right as he uses his left hand to push on the top grappler's head. As he does this, the bottom grappler starts to move his left foot and leg up and over the top grappler's head.

The bottom grappler drives his left foot and leg over his opponent's head, trapping it. As he does this, the bottom grappler slides his right hand up and over the top grappler's left arm, trapping it as well.

The bottom grappler forms the triangle with his feet and legs as shown. Look at the extreme side angle the bottom grappler has in relation to the top grappler. This is important to secure a strong triangle with the legs in this situation.

The bottom grappler secures the triangle choke as he uses his right hand and arm to trap and lock the top grappler's left arm. As he does this, the bottom grappler adds pressure to the choke by using his left hand to pull on the top grappler's right arm as shown.

#20 Head-Only Triangle Choke

Sometimes, using a triangle on only the head of the opponent gets the job done. This approach was used in the early days of professional wrestling by great wrestlers like Ed "Strangler" Lewis and others in the early part of the twentieth century. In some early catch wrestling circles, this move was known as the "Russian Headlock."

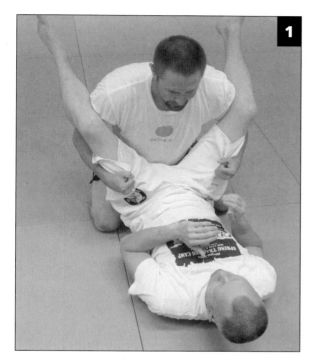

The top grappler is using both of his hands to grab the bottom grappler's legs in an attempt to pass his guard.

The bottom grappler uses his right hand to grab and hook the back of the top grappler's head. The bottom grappler uses his right hand to start to pull the top grappler's head down.

The bottom grappler uses both hands to grab and pull the top grappler's head down. As he does this, the bottom grappler moves his right foot and leg up and over the top grappler's left shoulder.

The bottom grappler continues to pull down on his opponent's head with both hands as he starts to form a triangle with his feet and leg. Look at how the bottom grappler has moved his left leg up and over the top grappler's right shoulder, forming the triangle on the head only (and not trapping the shoulder or arm).

The bottom grappler forms a tight triangle with his feet and legs around the top grappler's head. As he does this, the bottom grappler adds pressure to the move by continuing to use both hands to pull down on the top grappler's head.

#21 Ankle Choke from Bottom Guard

The bottom grappler has his opponent in his guard and has already moved his right foot and leg up and over the top grappler's left shoulder as shown. The bottom grappler uses both hands to trap and pull on the top grappler's right arm.

The bottom grappler moves his left foot and leg up as shown and will swing it over the top grappler's right arm and shoulder.

The bottom grappler positions his left foot over his opponent's right shoulder and jams his ankle directly under the top grappler's chin at his throat. As he does this, the bottom grappler moves his right foot and leg across the back of his opponent's head. Doing this traps the top grappler's head between the bottom grappler's left foot and right leg.

The bottom grappler uses his left hand to reach for his right ankle as shown. Look at how the bottom grappler's left foot and shin have been wedged tightly under his opponent's chin (at his throat).

The bottom grappler uses both hands to grab his lower right leg and drive it directly down. Doing this pulls the top grappler's head down and forward and drives his throat directly into the bottom grappler's left ankle and foot.

This view from the top shows how the bottom grappler exerts pressure to apply the choke.

#22 Ankle Choke with Head Pull from Bottom Guard

A variation of the ankle choke is for the bottom grappler to use both hands (though in some situations one may be enough to get the job done) to pull the top grappler's head down and forward.

#23 The Near-Hand Necktie

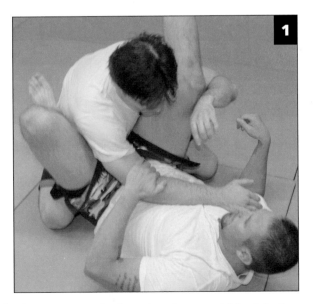

The bottom grappler has already moved his right leg up and over the top grappler's left arm and shoulder as shown.

The bottom grappler moves his right foot and leg around and behind the top grappler's head and neck. As he does this, the bottom grappler starts to use his right hand to reach for his right foot and leg.

The bottom grappler pushes down with his right foot and leg on his opponent's head as the bottom man uses his right hand to grab his right ankle. This traps the top grappler's head and neck, forming the "necktie." As he does this, the bottom grappler starts to move his left foot and leg up so he can form a triangle with his legs.

The bottom grappler forms a triangle with his legs. Doing this drives the top grappler's head down and forward and tighter into the necktie.

A variation of this choke is when the bottom grappler does not form a triangle with his legs and applies the necktie choke as shown in this photo.

#24 The Far-Hand Necktie

The bottom grappler has already moved his right foot and leg up and over the top grappler's left upper arm and shoulder as shown in this photo. As he does this, the bottom grappler start to use his left hand to reach out so he may be able to grab his right foot or ankle. The bottom grappler also starts to move his left foot and leg up to start to form a triangle with his legs. Look at how the bottom grappler uses his right hand to trap the top grappler's right arm.

The bottom grappler uses his left hand to grab his right shin or ankle as shown.

The bottom grappler uses his right foot and leg to drive down on the top grappler's head as the bottom man forms a triangle with his legs as shown. All the while he is doing this, the bottom grappler uses his left hand to help pull his right lower leg down harder on the back of the top man's neck. This forms a strong necktie choke.

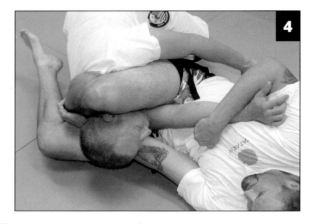

To make matters worse for the top grappler, the bottom grappler rolls to his left side. Doing this collapses the top grappler onto his right side allowing for a tighter necktie choke and triangle choke to be applied.

#25 Triangle Choke Escape from Side Hold

This is an old move that continues to have a good ratio of success. The bottom grappler is being held by his opponent with a *yoko shiho gatame* (side four-corner hold) or may even be controlled by an opponent with a strong side control position.

The bottom grappler uses his left hand to push on the left side of the top grappler's head to create some space and allow the bottom grappler to move his left leg.

The bottom grappler moves onto his right side slightly, and as he does this, he swings his left foot and leg up and over his opponent's head. At the same time, the bottom grappler uses his right hand and arm to hook under the top grappler's left arm as shown.

The bottom grappler moves his right foot and leg up and off the mat in order to form a triangle with his feet and legs. The bottom grappler uses both hands to secure a straight armlock on his opponent's extended left arm as shown.

The bottom grappler forms a strong triangle with his legs to apply the triangle choke as shown as he applies pressure with the straight armlock on the top grappler's left arm.

#26 Spinning Juji Gatame Attempt and Top Grappler Pulls Arm Out

The bottom grappler has his opponent in his guard and will attempt a spinning juji gatame (cross-body armlock).

TECHNICAL TIP: For more information on juji gatame, get a copy of *The Juji Gatame Encyclopedia* published by YMAA Publication Center.

The bottom grappler shrimps to his right as he starts to apply the spinning juji gatame.

The bottom grappler continues to spin under his opponent to apply juji gatame.

The top grappler starts to escape by stacking the bottom grappler high on his shoulder and upper back.

The top grappler manages to pull his right arm out from the armlock to make his escape.

The bottom grappler quickly spins back to his left and swings his left foot and leg up and over the top grappler's head. As he does this, the bottom grappler quickly uses both hands to grab onto the top man's left arm, trapping it to the bottom grappler's chest.

The bottom grappler moves his left foot and leg up and over the top grappler's right shoulder. After doing this, the bottom grappler uses his left foot and leg to drive down on the top grappler's head. The bottom grappler swings his right leg up in order to start to form a triangle.

The bottom grappler uses his left hand and arm to trap the top grappler's left arm as shown. As he does this, the bottom grappler uses his right hand to grab and pull on his left lower leg and form a triangle with his legs as shown.

The bottom grappler applies pressure with his legs, securing the triangle choke.

#27 Bent Armlock to Triangle Choke

The bottom grappler starts to apply a bent armlock from the bottom guard position.

The bottom grappler shrimps over onto his right hip and side as he starts to form the figure four with his hands and arms to secure the bent armlock.

This photo shows how the bottom grappler applies the bent armlock from this position, attacking the top grappler's left arm as shown.

For any number of reasons, the top grappler manages to move his left arm free and escape the bent armlock.

The bottom grappler immediately swings his right foot and leg up.

The bottom grappler swings his right foot and leg up and over the top grappler's left arm as shown. As he does this, the bottom grappler uses both of his hands to pull on his opponent's left upper arm. Doing this allows the bottom grappler to swing his right foot and leg up and over the top man's left arm more easily.

The bottom grappler continues to swing his right foot and leg up and over the top grappler's left arm and shoulder.

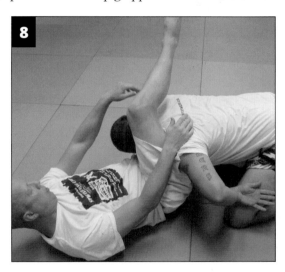

The bottom grappler uses his right foot and leg to clear his opponent's left shoulder as shown. As he does this, the bottom grappler uses his left hand to start to reach for his right foot or lower leg.

The bottom grappler uses his left hand to grab his right lower leg as shown, and as he does this, the bottom grappler uses his right hand to grab and pull his opponent's right arm as shown.

The bottom grappler moves his left foot and leg up and uses his left hand to grab and pull his right ankle and lower leg into the back of his left leg to form the triangle.

The triangle is formed and the bottom grappler applies pressure with his legs to secure the triangle choke.

#28 Bottom Grappler Starts with Triangle Choke and Switches to Juji Gatame

This is a good combination from a triangle choke to juji gatame (cross-body armlock).

The bottom grappler has his opponent in a triangle choke as shown.

The top grappler manages to pull his head out and free of the triangle choke. The bottom grappler quickly moves his left leg over the head of the top grappler as shown. The bottom grappler also uses both hands to trap his opponent's right arm to the bottom man's chest.

The bottom grappler shifts to his right and forces the top grappler to collapse as shown. As he does this, the bottom grappler uses both his hand and arms to pull his opponent's right arm straight. The bottom grappler also makes sure to arch his hips to add pressure to the elbow, forcing the tap out.

For more combinations to juji gatame, refer to *The Juji Gatame Encyclopedia* published by YMAA Publication Center.

#29 Double Arm Triangle Choke

top grappler's arms in tighter. Look at how the bottom grappler traps the top man's shoulders and squeezes them together.

The bottom grappler uses both of his hands to grab and trap his opponent's forearms to his chest as shown. As he does this, the bottom grappler starts to move his legs to start his triangle. Look at how the bottom grappler is moving his right leg up and over the top grappler's left arm and shoulder.

The bottom man starts to move to his right side and uses his right hand and arm to hook under the top grappler's left leg as shown.

As he starts to form his triangle with his feet and legs, the bottom grappler uses both of his hands to pull the

The bottom grappler has positioned his body so that it is at a sideways angle to his opponent as shown. As he moves to his right and uses his right hand and arm to hook under his opponent's left leg to roll him over, the bottom grappler forms a tight triangle with his legs, trapping the top grappler's arms. The bottom grappler has formed a strong triangle choke as well, trapping both of the top grappler's arms. At this point, the top grappler is controlled with both the triangle choke and a double arm juji gatame (cross-body armlock).

The bottom grappler rolls his opponent over onto his side as shown and applies both the triangle choke and armlock in this double trouble situation.

#30 Guillotine Choke to Triangle Choke

The bottom grappler is fighting his opponent from the bottom guard as shown.

The bottom grappler reaches up with his right hand and arm and attacks the top grappler with a guillotine choke.

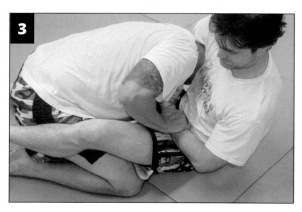

The top grappler uses his right hand to grab and pull the attacker's left hand to ease the pressure form the guillotine choke.

The bottom grappler moves his left foot and leg up as he continues to control his opponent's head with the guillotine.

The bottom grappler moves his left foot and leg up and over his opponent's right upper arm and shoulder.

The bottom grappler slides his right arm down from the top grappler's head. As he does this, the bottom grappler moves his left foot and leg over and behind the top grappler's head. The bottom grappler uses his left hand to help pull his left foot and ankle lower to trap the top man's head.

The bottom grappler uses his right hand to let go of his opponent's head as shown in this photo. The bottom grappler will use his right hand to grab the top grappler's left elbow.

The bottom grappler uses his right hand to grab his opponent's left elbow and pulls up on it to control it. As he does this, the bottom grappler swings his right foot and leg up to form the triangle.

The bottom grappler forms the triangle with his feet and legs as he continues to use his right hand to pull on his opponent's left elbow.

The triangle has been formed and the bottom grappler adds pressure to the choke by using both of his hands to grab and pull his left lower leg down onto the back of his opponent's head and neck.

#31 Guillotine to Near Leg Triangle Choke

The bottom grappler attempts a guillotine choke from the bottom guard.

For any number of reasons, the guillotine choke doesn't work. The bottom grappler moves his right foot and leg up and over the top grappler's left upper arm and shoulder.

The bottom grappler lets go from around his opponent's head and neck with his right hand and uses it to grab his right ankle or lower leg.

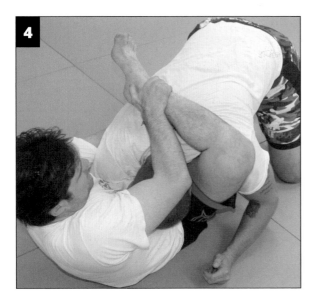

The bottom grappler uses his right hand to grab and pull his right leg down as shown.

The bottom grappler moves his left foot and leg up to start to form the triangle.

The bottom grappler moves his left foot up and forms the triangle as shown. Look at how the bottom grappler has trapped the top grappler's right shoulder as well as his head.

The bottom grappler forms his triangle and secures the triangle choke to get the tap out.

#32 Bottom Grappler Spins into Top Grappler to Tighten the Triangle Choke

This is an effective and often-used method to sink in the triangle choke and make it tighter.

The bottom grappler applies a triangle choke from the straight-on position but the top grappler is not tapping out.

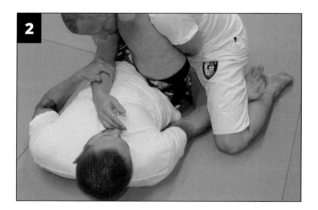

To tighten the choke, the bottom grappler must re-position his body so that he can create a tighter squeezing action with his legs. To do this, the bottom grappler moves to his right and uses his right hand and arm to hook under and grab his opponent's left leg as shown.

The bottom grappler has moved his body to his right so that it is now in a side angle in relation to his opponent. Look at how the bottom grappler has moved his head in close to his opponent's left knee.

The bottom grappler is now positioned so that he can create a stronger triangle with his legs to secure the choke. The bottom grappler also uses his left hand to control his opponent's right arm to secure the armlock.

#33 Triangle Choke for Short Legs

In a lot of situations, athletes with short legs tend to shy away from using triangle chokes, so this variation may be useful for them.

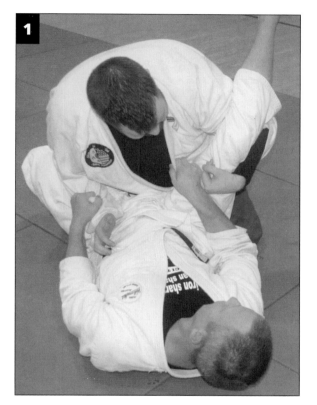

The bottom grappler is fighting his opponent from the bottom guard as shown.

The bottom grappler's goal is to spin or move to his right so that his head is as close as possible to the top grappler's left knee or leg as shown. Moving the body to the side in this way makes the bottom grappler's legs "longer." What it actually does is allow the bottom grappler a better position to use his short legs to his advantage. Look at how the bottom grappler uses his right leg to clear the top grappler's left shoulder and jam it forcefully on the left side of the top grappler's neck.

The bottom grappler forms a triangle by doing his best to place his right ankle or the top of his right foot in the back of his knee. This probably won't be possible because of the bottom grappler's short legs, so he can place the top of his right foot on the back of his left calf muscle instead. Doing this forms a tight triangle. Look at how the bottom grappler controls his opponent by using his right hand and arm to grab the top grappler's left leg and how the bottom grappler uses his left hand to grab and trap the top grappler's right arm.

The bottom grappler rolls his opponent over as shown.

This photo shows how the short legs of the bottom grappler have been effectively used as the bottom grappler rolls the top grappler over onto his side.

This photo shows how the bottom grappler's legs have extended because of the side angle of the attack. This "lengthening" of the legs helps a short-legged fighter secure a tighter triangle choke.

#34 Triangle Choke for Heavyweights

In a good many cases, heavyweight grapplers have some trouble forming a triangle because of the thickness of their legs and the thickness of their opponent's body.

The bottom grappler has his opponent in his guard as shown.

The bottom grappler spins to his left. To help his body move in that direction, the bottom grappler uses his left hand to grab his opponent's right leg and pulls himself in the direction of the opponent's right leg. Doing this creates a side angle as shown and greatly helps the bottom grappler extend his anchor leg (his left leg in this photo) to clear the top man's right shoulder and jam the left leg in the right side of the top grappler's neck.

The bottom grappler uses his right leg to form the triangle as shown. As he does this, the bottom grappler rolls to his right side as he uses his left hand to hook under his opponent's right leg and lift it. Doing this forces the top grappler to topple forward and onto his left side as shown. This extends or "lengthens" the bottom grappler's right leg, making the formation of the triangle easier and more effective.

The bottom grappler continues to roll onto his right side. The rolling action (to the right in this photo) by the bottom grappler allows him to tighten his triangle with his legs to secure a stronger choke.

TECHNICAL TIP: By rolling to his side and forcing his opponent to do the same, the bottom grappler's girth and leg thickness are less cumbersome in forming the triangle choke.

#35 Switch Triangle from One Side to the Other

The bottom grappler attempts a triangle choke with his right foot and leg initially placed over the top grappler's left shoulder, but the top grappler uses his right hand and arm to push the bottom man's leg away to prevent the triangle from being formed. As all this takes place, the bottom grappler immediately swings his left foot and leg up and over the right upper arm and shoulder of the top grappler as shown.

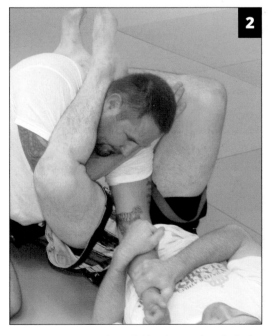

The bottom grappler forcefully drives his left foot and lower leg down and onto the top grappler's neck and head. What was originally the bottom grappler's tie-up leg (the left leg) is now his anchor leg to form the triangle.

The bottom grappler uses his right leg as the tie-up leg as he forms a triangle by placing his left foot and ankle on the inside of his right knee as shown. For more control, the bottom grappler uses both of his hands to grab and pull the top grappler's left arm as shown.

The bottom grappler forms a tight triangle choke to get the tap out.

#36 Lapel-Style Triangle Choke

This is a technique that comes directly from Kosen judo and is popular in all forms of grappling where a jacket is used such as judo and BJJ.

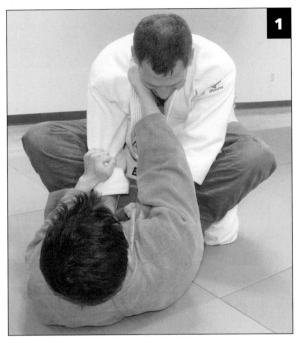

The bottom grappler uses both of his feet to wedge in the top grappler's hips. As he does this, the bottom grappler uses his right hand to reach in and grab the top grappler's left lapel as shown. The bottom grappler uses his left hand to grab the top man's right sleeve or arm.

The bottom grappler uses his right leg to slide up and over the top grappler's left arm and shoulder. The bottom grappler makes it a point to drive his right upper leg hard against the left side of the top grappler's neck.

The bottom grappler uses his right leg to drive against the top man's neck and head as he uses his right hand to pull down on the lapel of the top man's jacket. All the while, the bottom grappler continues to use his left hand to pull on the extended right arm of the top grappler.

The bottom grappler starts to form the triangle with his legs as he continues to use his right hand to pull downward on the top grappler's lapel.

The bottom grappler may use his left hand to grab his right lower leg or ankle and place his right foot and ankle under his left knee as shown. As he does this, the bottom grappler continues to use his right hand to pull downward on the top man's lapel. The combination of the squeezing action of the legs in the triangle and the trapping and pulling of the right hand on the lapel creates a strong choke.

The bottom grappler continues to squeeze with his legs that formed the triangle and pull with his right hand on the top grappler's lapel jacket to get the tap out.

#37 Meathook Grip to Secure the "Head Only" Triangle Choke

Triangle chokes controlling only the head (and not the shoulder or arm) of the opponent are effective, but many grappling sports don't allow them. However, these triangle chokes work, so my advice is to learn them and use them whenever possible.

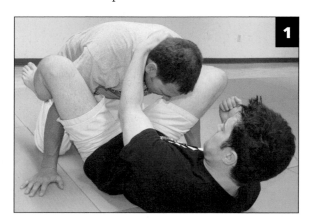

The bottom grappler uses his left hand to grab and hook on the back of his opponent's head, pulling it down as shown. As he does this, the bottom grappler starts to move his right foot and leg up to begin to form a triangle.

The bottom grappler moves his right foot and leg up and over the top grappler's left shoulder. As he does this, the bottom grappler continues to pull down with his left hand on the top grappler's head. The bottom grappler moves his left leg up and over the top grappler's right upper arm and shoulder to start to form a triangle.

The bottom grappler starts to form a triangle with his feet and legs around the top grappler's head. As he does this, the bottom grappler has firm control with his left hand as it hooks the top grappler's head. The bottom grappler's left hand is on the right side of the top man's neck at the carotid artery area.

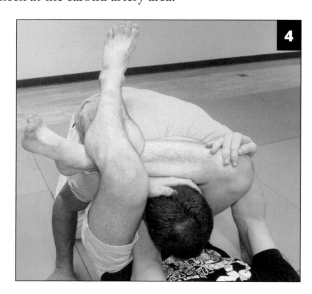

Look at how the bottom grappler's left hand is on the right side of the top man's neck at the carotid artery area. Doing this adds more pressure (creating a stronger strangling action) to the triangle formed with the leg around the top grappler's head.

The bottom grappler uses his legs to squeeze the top grappler's head as the bottom grappler jams his left hand on the right side of the top grappler's neck (and continues to pull the top man's head down with his left hand as well). Doing this causes a strong strangling action and gets the tap out.

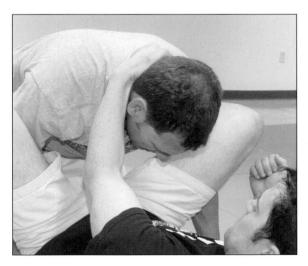

TECHNICAL TIP: A "MEATHOOK"
A "meathook" is a quick grab and hooking motion where the hand is used to hook onto a particular part of the body (either the opponent's

body part or the attacker's own body part) and pull to better control or manipulate the part of the body that has been "meathooked." The meathook has also been called a "hook and pull." This photo shows the bottom grappler using his left hand to "meathook" the top grappler's head.

#38 Body Triangle with Shoulder Choke

Sometimes a body triangle can be used to either control an opponent or to apply pressure to the opponent's torso, forcing him to submit to the pressure. In this situation, the bottom grappler wants to do both as he also applies a kata jime (shoulder choke), also known as an "arm triangle choke."

The bottom grappler has his opponent in his guard.

The bottom grappler uses his left hand to grab and pull the top grappler's left arm across the bottom grappler's body as shown.

The bottom grappler pulls the top grappler's left arm across so that the bottom man's head is positioned on the outside of the top man's left arm and shoulder as shown. As he does this, the bottom grappler moves his left foot up and uses his right hand to reach over the back of his opponent to start to grab his left ankle or foot.

The bottom grappler uses his right hand to firmly grab his left ankle as shown. As he does this, the bottom grappler uses his left hand to grab and pull the top grappler's extended left arm so that the bottom grappler can more easily move to his right and to the outside of the top man's left shoulder as shown.

The bottom grappler forms a triangle with his feet and legs around the torso (below the ribs of the top grappler).

The bottom grappler grasps his hands together to form a shoulder choke (also called an arm triangle) as the bottom grappler applies pressure with the triangle formed by his feet and legs.

The bottom grappler has his opponent in double trouble with both a shoulder choke and a body triangle. Even if the body triangle doesn't force the top grappler to submit, it controls him so the shoulder choke can be effectively applied.

#39 Arm Trap Body Triangle with Cross Lapel Choke

The bottom grappler uses his right hand to grab and control the top grappler's left forearm.

The bottom grappler uses his right hand to push the top grappler's left arm back, and as he does this, the bottom grappler starts to move his right foot and leg up. As he does this, the bottom grappler uses his left hand to grab the top grappler's left jacket lapel.

The bottom grappler uses his right leg to trap the top grappler's left arm as shown.

The bottom grappler uses his right hand to grab the top grappler's left jacket lapel and pulls it out so that the bottom grappler can now use his left hand to reach deeply on the inside of the top man's left lapel and grab it. As he does this, the bottom grappler forms a triangle with his legs, trapping the top grappler's left arm to the side of his body as shown. The bottom grappler now controls the top grappler with this body triangle so that the bottom grappler can more effectively secure the cross choke on the lapels.

This view from the top shows how the bottom grappler uses the body triangle to trap his opponent. The bottom grappler applies a cross choke using the lapels of his opponent's jacket.

The bottom grappler slides his right hand under the top grappler's chin and uses his right hand to grab onto the inside of the top man's right lapel. The bottom grappler reaches and grabs deeply into the top grappler's lapels so that a strong cross lapel choke will be formed.

The bottom grappler controls the top grappler with the body triangle as he applies a strong cross lapel choke to get the tap out.

#40 Ankle Choke with a Necktie

The bottom grappler controls his opponent from the bottom guard.

The bottom grappler moves his right foot and leg up and over the top grappler's left shoulder.

The bottom grappler uses his left hand to start to grab his right ankle.

The bottom grappler uses his left hand to grab his right ankle and start to move his right foot and lower leg over the back and top of the top grappler's head.

The bottom grappler quickly uses his right hand to grab and hook on the back of the top grappler's neck and head, pulling it down. As he does this, the bottom grappler continues to move his right lower leg over the top man's head as shown.

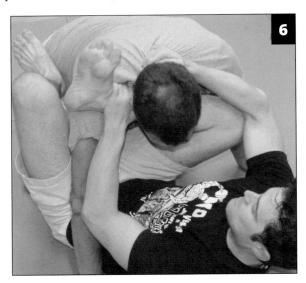

The bottom grappler jams his right ankle and shin up and into the throat of the top grappler as shown. As he does this, the bottom grappler continues to use his right hand to pull down and control the opponent's head, keeping the top grappler from "posturing up" or sitting erect to escape the choke.

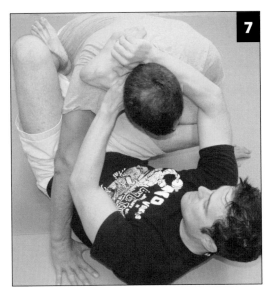

The bottom grappler quickly uses his right hand to grab the instep (or the toes on the inside) of his right foot as shown. Doing this traps the top grappler's head between the bottom grappler's right shin and right forearm. The bottom grappler's right hand and right shin form a strong "necktie" around the top grappler's head, creating a nasty choke.

The bottom grappler uses his right forearm to press against the left side of the top grappler's neck at the carotid artery. This creates a strong choke. To add more pressure to the choke, the bottom grappler uses his left foot to push against the top grappler's shoulder.

As mentioned previously, there are a lot of variations of the triangle choke from the bottom guard, so take what you see in this book and get creative. Now let's examine the triangle choke starting from the front of an opponent or from a neutral starting position.

"Everybody's got a neck!"
Dewey Mitchell

Part 3: Triangle Chokes
When in Front of an Opponent

TRIANGLE CHOKES WHEN THE ATTACKER IS IN FRONT OF AN OPPONENT

Two common methods of applying triangle chokes that have evolved over the years are used when the defender is either kneeling or prone on the mat or when both fighters are facing each other in a neutral position (either on the knees or standing). In any event, the attacker is positioned so that he is in front of his opponent.

In some situations, the defender may be positioned so that he is lying on his front, kneeling on hands and knees, or balled up as tightly as he can; in all of these cases, his goal is to somehow (usually mistakenly) survive the onslaught of the attacker (often in the hope of having the referee call a halt to the action). In some cases, this defensive position may work, but in a lot of instances, it's simply a chance for a skilled grappler to secure a triangle choke and get the tap out. This approach was initially used in Kosen judo in the early part of the twentieth century and has developed over the years in all levels of modern judo, submission grappling, and BJJ competition.

In other instances, both grapplers are facing each other in a neutral position, either on the knees or standing. In this situation, the attacker should have a definite plan as to how he will set his opponent up or place him in a vulnerable position from this neutral situation. This form of a front-starting position presents more challenges to the attacker as his opponent often has as much freedom of movement or mobility initially as the attacker does. In these situations, the attacker needs to have an effective and well-rehearsed method of setting his opponent up or breaking his opponent down so that the attacker can secure the triangle choke.

So then, this chapter will examine the triangle chokes that can be used in either of these situations. A wide variety of triangle choke applications coming from these front-starting positions will be presented, but obviously not every move ever invented can be included. So use your imagination to expand on what is shown on the following pages.

THE TWO BASIC APPROACHES TO ATTACKING AN OPPONENT FROM THE FRONT

There are two basic approaches when attacking an opponent from the front. They are:

1. The "front ride" start where the attacker is standing or kneeling at the head of his opponent who is already on the mat and either positioned on all fours or lying on his front.
2. The "neutral" start where the attacker is either standing or kneeling facing his opponent who is either standing or kneeling as well.

ATTACKING AN OPPONENT FROM THE FRONT RIDE STARTING POSITION

In this first approach for a front attack, the attacker is standing or kneeling at the head of his opponent who is positioned on hands and knees, balled up tightly, or lying flat on his front.

THE DEFENDER IS ON ALL FOURS (IN A GI SITUATION)

The attacker stands and the defender is positioned on all fours on hands (or elbows) and knees as shown. This is a fairly common position in just about all of the fighting sports. This photo shows the defender on his elbows and knees.

THE DEFENDER IS ON ALL FOURS (IN A NO-GI SITUATION)

This photo shows the defender on his hands and knees in a "parterre" position from wrestling.

THE DEFENDER IS BALLED UP TIGHT

The defender is on all fours, balled up tightly with his hands, arms, feet, and legs in as close to his body as possible. The defender is in an extremely defensive position with the goal being to survive the top fighter's attack and hope for the referee to call a halt to the action, giving him a reprieve.

THE DEFENDER IS LYING FLAT ON HIS FRONT

Another extreme defensive position is when the defender lies flat on his front and tries to get as flat as possible on the mat in the hope that the attacker will not be able to secure a submission technique or turn the defender over onto his back. Usually what takes place is that the attacker pretty much has his way with the defender and gets a tap out.

ATTACKING AN OPPONENT WHEN IN THE NEUTRAL FRONT STARTING POSITION

In this second approach to front triangle attacks, the attacker and defender are facing each other in either a kneeling or a standing start position.

BOTH GRAPPLERS ARE IN A NEUTRAL KNEELING POSITION

This photo shows a common situation where both grapplers are kneeling (on both knees or on one knee) and tied up in a grip of some type. Both grapplers are in a neutral position in relation to each other at this point of the match.

THE ATTACKER IS STANDING AND THE DEFENDER IS KNEELING

The attacker is standing and his opponent is kneeling on both knees or on one knee. The attacker often has the advantage in this situation as he has more freedom of movement.

BOTH THE ATTACKER AND DEFENDER ARE FACING EACH OTHER BUT HAVE NOT MADE CONTACT

This is a neutral position with both fighters squared off, standing and facing each other. They have not made contact with each other at this point.

BOTH THE ATTACKER AND DEFENDER ARE STANDING AND HAVE MADE CONTACT (EITHER A GRIP, TIE-UP, OR CLINCH)

The grapplers are standing and have gripped each other or secured a tie-up but are in a neutral position at this point.

THE COMMON FINISH POSITIONS FOR A FRONT ATTACK

This was discussed in the first chapter of this book, but it's not a bad idea to review it again in this chapter, so it's at this point that a little historical perspective is in order to better explain the most common finish positions for the triangle choke, especially as it is applied from a front ride or front neutral starting position. As explained in the introduction to this book, the historical or "traditional" method of classifying triangle chokes has been in the context or perspective of how the choke is finished. This has offered a good explanation of the conclusion, but didn't satisfactorily explain how the grapplers or fighters ended up where they were and how the choke was started or applied.

The front starting position (whether it's from the front ride position or from the front neutral position) provides a variety of finishing positions with the four most common being:

1. The attacker finishes the choke when lying in a side position relative to his opponent.
2. The attacker finishes the choke when positioned in a reverse (upside down or north-south) position relative to his opponent.
3. The attacker finishes the choke when positioned behind his opponent.
4. The attacker finishes the choke when in front and facing his opponent. The four most common finish positions are presented with the Japanese terminology that has historically been applied to them.

Remember, what matters most is that the attacker controls his opponent and secures the triangle choke. How the attacker finishes the choke is less important than how successful he is in applying and executing it. How the attacker executes the choke is often determined by how well he controls the position and controls his opponent initially. The old saying, "Control the position and get the submission" is certainly true in this case.

There are numerous other finish positions that will be presented in this chapter, but these four are probably the most common.

YOKO SANKAKU JIME (SIDE TRIANGLE CHOKE)

The attacker lies on his side as he applies the triangle choke.

GYAKU SANKAKU JIME (REVERSE TRIANGLE CHOKE)

The attacker is in a north-south position relative to the defender in this application of the triangle choke.

URA SANKAKU JIME (REAR TRIANGLE CHOKE)

The attacker applies the triangle choke from behind the defender in this variation.

OMOTE SANKAKU JIME (FRONT-FACING TRIANGLE CHOKE)

The attacker faces (or is positioned in front of) the defender as he applies this variation of the triangle choke.

THE PRIMARY PARTS OF A TRIANGLE CHOKE FROM THE FRONT START POSITION

Years of experience in a variety of combat sports and thousands of matches have proven that executing a triangle choke from the top ride position is a common and effective method of performing the triangle choke. There is a specific series of actions that the attacker performs in this approach to securing the triangle choke from this position. These specific actions have been broken down into four major parts.

1. The attacker ties up, closes the space between his body and the defender's body, and controls the defender's upper body.
2. The attacker turns the defender onto his side or back.
3. The attacker traps the defender's arms and upper body.
4. The attacker forms the triangle with his feet and legs and applies pressure.

THE FIRST PART: ATTACKER TIES UP THE DEFENDER'S UPPER BODY AND CLOSES THE SPACE BETWEEN THEIR BODIES

The attacker (top grappler) uses his legs to (1) control the arms and upper body of the defender (bottom grappler) and (2) close the distance or space between the attacker's body and the defender's body.

The Attacker Uses His Legs to Control His Opponent's Upper Body

The attacker is positioned in front of the defender and is on his knees in this photo.

The attacker (the top grappler) drives his right knee and upper leg onto the left shoulder of the defender. This closes the space between the two grapplers and is an important first step.

TECHNICAL TIP: The attacker must close the space between his body and the bottom grappler's body, and this is an ideal way of closing the body space.

The attacker uses his left foot and leg to hook over the right upper arm and shoulder of the defender.

The attacker uses his left foot and leg to hook under the defender's right armpit as shown. The attacker's goal is to have his left heel touch his right knee at this point of the attack. Doing this securely traps the bottom grappler's upper body, especially his head, right shoulder, and right arm. The attacker will proceed to apply the triangle choke from this initial controlling position.

This photo shows the attacker's right upper leg and hip jammed solidly against the defender's left shoulder, and the attacker's left foot and leg hooked over the bottom grappler's right shoulder. Doing this gives the attacker good control of his opponent's upper body and sets the bottom grappler up for the roll into the triangle choke.

The Attacker Uses His Hands and Arms to Control Opponent's Upper Body

There are numerous "handles" on everyone's body that can be grabbed, hooked, or used for control. The attacker uses his hands and arms to control his opponent's upper body to help in closing the distance between himself and his opponent in preparation for turning the bottom grappler over onto his back to further secure the triangle. Presented here are a few ways the attacker can use the handles of the defender's body, arms, jacket, or belt (or anything else) for maximum control.

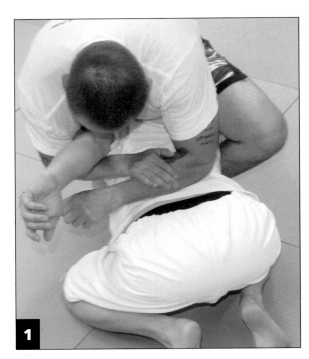

The top grappler uses his right hand and arm to hook under the defender's left arm and shoulder to control the bottom grappler's upper body.

The top grappler uses his left hand to grab and control his opponent's right sleeve at the elbow. The attacker uses his right hand to grab the bottom grappler's belt. Doing this gives the attacker two good "handles" to better control his opponent as he turns the bottom grappler over onto his side or back.

The attacker uses both hands to grab the bottom grappler's belt. The attacker uses the belt to help pull the bottom grappler over onto his side or back.

Sometimes, the attacker will use his hands and arms to hug or grab the bottom grappler's torso, hips, or even legs as a handle to better control him.

THE SECOND PART: ATTACKER TURNS THE DEFENDER ONTO HIS BACK OR SIDE

After closing the distance between himself and his opponent, the attacker's next step is to control the bottom grappler's body as the attacker rolls onto his side, pulling the defender over onto the defender's side and back.

The Attacker Rolls onto His Side and Rolls His Opponent Over onto His Side and Back

As the attacker controls the defender and closes the space between his body and the defender's body, the attacker will use his feet and legs to hook and control the defender and turn the bottom grappler onto his side or back. From there, the attacker will secure the triangle position more securely with his feet and legs.

The attacker (top grappler) has positioned his right foot and leg so that it hooks and controls the bottom grappler as shown in this photo. If the grapplers are wearing jackets and belts, the attacker will use his hands to grab and control the bottom grappler's belt and jacket as shown.

The top grappler rolls to his right side, pulling the bottom grappler over to his left.

The top grappler has rolled to his right side (not onto his back, but directly onto his right side). In doing this, the top grappler has pulled his opponent over onto his right side and onto his back.

THE THIRD PART: ATTACKER TRAPS THE DEFENDER'S ARMS AND UPPER BODY AFTER TURNING HIM ONTO HIS SIDE OR BACK

The attacker uses his top leg to control the defender's far arm as he uses his hands and arms to trap and control the defender's near arm.

Drag and Pull: The Attacker Drags the Defender's Far or Top Arm in with His Leg and Pulls the Defender's Far or Top Arm

When the attacker traps, isolates, and controls his opponent's arms, he does so in two phases. The initial phase is for the attacker to use his top foot and leg (in this photo series, it's the attacker's left foot and leg) to hook and "drag" or pull the defender's far arm (in this photo series, it's the defender's left arm). The attacker does this to prevent the bottom grappler from using his arm to pull out and away from the triangle that is in the process of forming. Doing this also allows the attacker more control to cinch the triangle in tighter as it is forming.

Attacker Uses His Top Foot and Leg to Hook and Control the Defender's Top Arm

Now that the top grappler has pulled his opponent over onto his back, the top grappler uses his top foot and leg (in this photo, his left foot and leg) to hook and control the bottom grappler's right arm. Look at how the top grappler uses his left foot and lower leg to hook and manipulate the bottom grappler's left upper arm.

The top grappler uses his left foot and lower leg to hook and pull his opponent's left upper arm in tightly.

By manipulating the bottom grappler's left upper arm, the top grappler is better able to place his left foot in the back of his right knee and form a triangle as shown in this photo.

This photo shows how the attacker uses his left foot and leg to hook at the triceps area of the defender to secure a tighter hooking action with his leg.

Attacker Pulls Defender's Top Arm in Tight

To really cinch in the triangle with the foot and legs, the attacker will use her (in this series of photos) right hand to grab the defender's top (right) arm and pull the arm in tightly. Doing this allows the attacker to better hook the defender's top arm to pull it in more tightly, creating a strong and tight triangle.

There are several effective ways for the attacker to grab, hook, and pull the defender's top arm in securely.

The attacker uses her right hand to grab the defender's right wrist as she uses her right foot and leg to hook and pull on the bottom grappler's right upper arm.

The attacker uses her right hand to grab onto the defender's right wrist or lower arm and pull it.

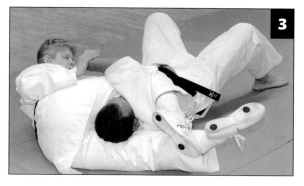

The attacker has used her right hand to pull the defender's right arm across his body as the attacker forms a tight triangle with her feet and legs.

Attacker Pulls on Defender's Wrist

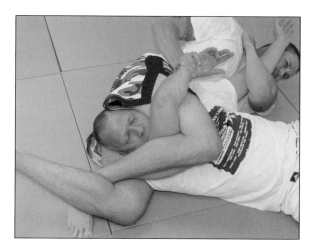

In this no-gi situation, the defender uses his right hand to grab and pull on the defender's right wrist.

Attacker Pulls on Defender's Sleeve

In a situation where the sport allows jackets, the attacker can use his hand (in this photo, his left hand) to grab his opponent's left sleeve to get a better grip and pull the arm in tightly.

Attacker Pulls on Defender's Elbow

The attacker can use her right hand to grab and scoop the defender's right elbow in tightly. Grabbing and scooping the defender's elbow is an effective way to cinch in the defender's arm tightly to secure the triangle with the legs. In this application, the attacker's right hand is positioned with her thumb up.

This photo shows the attacker using his right hand to grab and pull the defender's right elbow. In this application, the attacker's right hand is positioned with his thumb down.

Attacker Applies a Bent Armlock on Defender's Top Arm

This is a classic case of "double trouble" with the attacker applying both the triangle choke and a bent armlock at the same time.

The attacker uses her right hand to grab and control the defender's right wrist. The attacker has firm control of her opponent with her triangle hold as she does this.

The attacker uses her right hand to push the defender's bent right arm toward his belt area. Doing this creates a strong and painful bent armlock (*ude garami*). This is an effective and common "double trouble" situation.

Attacker Applies a Wrist Lock on the Defender's Top Arm

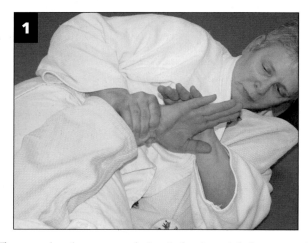

The attacker has trapped the defender with her triangle and uses her right hand to grab the defender's right wrist, making sure to hold and isolate it. As she does this, the attacker uses his right hand to start to grab the defender's right hand as shown.

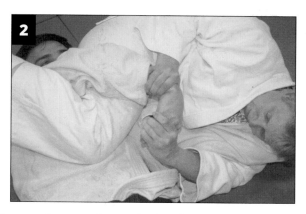

The attacker uses her right hand to grab the fingers of the defender's right hand as shown. The attacker uses her right hand to hold and control the defender's right wrist as the attacker bends the defender's right hand downward, creating a wristlock.

The Attacker Traps and Controls the Defender's Near or Bottom Arm for Control

As the attacker traps his opponent's far or top arm, the attacker must also trap and control the defender's arm that is nearer to the attacker (this is usually the defender's bottom arm). Trapping the defender's near or bottom arm really helps the attacker in controlling his opponent so that he has time to secure a tight triangle with his feet and legs. There are several effective and common methods of doing this that will be presented here.

One-Arm Hug Trap

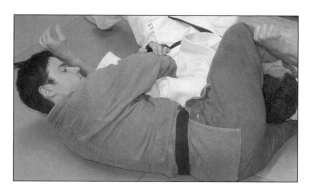

This is a quick and secure way for the attacker to trap the defender's near or bottom arm. The attacker simply uses one hand and arm (in this photo, the attacker's right arm) to hook and trap the defender's left arm.

Both-Arm Hug Trap

The attacker uses both of his hands and arms to grab and trap the defender's near (in this photo, the left) arm tightly to the attacker's torso.

Hug-and-Grab Shoulder Trap

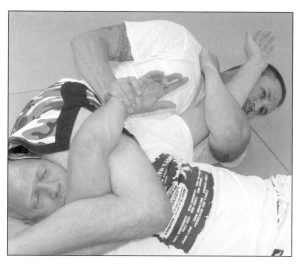

The attacker uses his left arm to hook and trap the defender's left arm tightly to the attacker's chest as shown.

Attacker Traps Defender's Bottom Arm with His Body as He Uses His Bottom Hand and Arm to Control Defender's Near Leg

The attacker positions his body so that he uses his bottom (in this photo, his left) hand to grab the defender's near (in this photo, left) leg. Doing this, the attacker traps the defender's bottom arm (the left arm in this photo) with his body as he gains a lot of control with his left hand and arm that has trapped the defender's left leg as shown. This is a tight and secure application of the triangle choke.

Keylock Trap for Defender's Bottom Arm

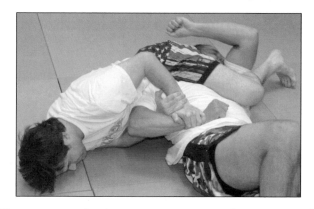

The top grappler has a secure trap on his opponent's bottom (right) arm as shown. This can often lead to a bent armlock as well.

Bent Armlock Trap and Triple Trouble

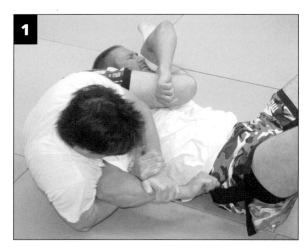

The top grappler can turn the keylock trap into a bent armlock by using both hands to yank the defender's bent (right) arm away from the defender's body as shown.

The attacker applies pressure to the armlock by turning to face the mat and cranking downward with his arms and the momentum of his body turning toward the mat as shown. This is an ideal "triple trouble" situation where the top grappler has a triangle choke, a pin, and a bent armlock on his opponent.

Judo Keylock with Jacket Apron (Suso Gatame-Apron Hold)

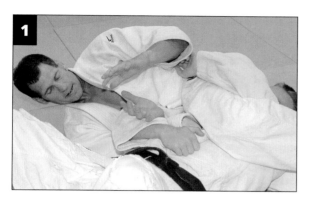

A common and effective way of controlling the defender's near arm is for the attacker to use a "judo keylock." The attacker uses his right hand to trap the defender's right lower arm in this photo.

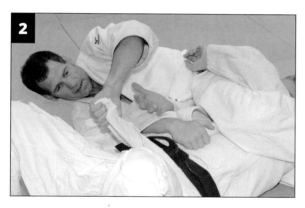

The attacker uses his left hand to grab the apron or bottom of the defender's jacket and pull it over the defender's right forearm as shown.

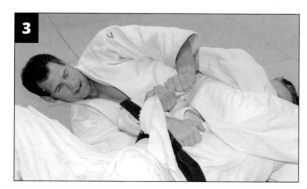

The attacker uses his left hand to grab the apron of the defender's jacket and pull it in tightly to the defender's body, trapping it.

Judo Keylock with Belt (Obi Gatame-Belt Hold)

The attacker uses his left hand to trap the defender's right forearm to the defender's body as shown. As he does this, the attacker uses his left hand to reach over and grab the defender's belt.

The attacker uses his left hand to grab the defender's belt. As he does this, the attacker starts to pull the belt over the defender's trapped right wrist and forearm.

The attacker uses his right hand to grab and hold the defender's belt tightly over the defender's right wrist and forearm, trapping it tightly to the defender's body.

THE FOURTH PART: THE ATTACKER FORMS THE TRIANGLE AND APPLIES PRESSURE

The attacker has turned the defender onto his back and then forms the triangle with his feet and legs to control his opponent and then apply pressure and tighten the strangle with his feet and legs to get the tap out.

The attacker is lying on his right side and uses his top leg (his left leg in this photo) to hook and pull the defender's left arm in tightly. The attacker extends his bottom leg (his right leg in this photo) out straight so that the defender's head is positioned on the attacker's leg as shown.

The attacker places his left foot on the inside of his right knee, forming the triangle. As he does this, the attacker uses his left hand to grab and pull the defender's left arm in tight. Doing this forms a tight triangle.

TECHNICAL TIP: The attacker uses his bottom leg (in this photo, his right leg) that is lying on the mat as a "pillow" for the defender's head. The defender's head and neck lie on the defender's extended leg as shown. Doing this ensures that the attacker has his opponent's head placed correctly and securely and can better form the triangle with his other foot and leg.

Attacker's Control of Both of His Opponent's Arms Is not Always Necessary

It may not always be necessary for the attacker to control both of the defender's arms in order to apply an effective triangle choke. Here are three situations where the attacker controls only one (or neither) of the defender's arms when applying the triangle choke.

Attacker Has Control of Defender's Near (Bottom) Arm but not His Far (Top) Arm

The attacker has control of his opponent's near (left) arm with a both-arm hug but does not have control of the defender's far (right) arm. The triangle that the attacker has formed with his feet and legs is strong enough to secure an effective choke.

Attacker Has Control of the Defender's Far (Top) Arm but not His Near (Bottom) Arm

The attacker uses his right hand and arm to pull and control the defender's far arm (in this photo, the defender's right arm). In this situation, the attacker does not trap the defender's near (her left) arm with his left hand or arm and can use the close proximity of his body to trap the arm (if it is trapped at all).

Attacker Does not Control Either of His Opponent's Arms to Secure the Triangle Choke

In some cases (as shown in this photo) the attacker secures a strong triangle choke without using either hand to control his opponent.

Up to this point, the different parts of the triangle have been analyzed. Let's now examine some useful applications and variations to secure a triangle choke when the attacker is positioned in front of an opponent.

#1 Front Attack When Opponent Is on Elbows and Knees (Wearing Judo or Jujitsu Jackets)

The top grappler stands over his opponent who is on elbows and knees.

The attacker closes the space between his body and the bottom grappler's body and uses his right foot to step over and hook the bottom grappler's left arm.

This photo shows how the top grappler places his left knee on the mat and places his left upper leg firmly on the bottom grappler's right shoulder. The top grappler does this as he steps in with his right foot and leg as shown in photo #2. Look at how the top grappler uses his left hand to grab and control the bottom grappler's right sleeve at his elbow.

The attacker firmly hooks his right foot in under the bottom grappler's left armpit. Doing this traps the bottom grappler's left arm and shoulder as shown. As he does this, the top grappler uses his right hand to grab the bottom man's belt.

The top grappler rolls to his right, and as he does, he pulls the bottom grappler as shown.

The top grappler has rolled onto his right side, pulling his opponent over onto his back as shown.

The attacker lies on his left side as shown and uses his left foot and leg to hook and control the bottom grappler's left upper arm as shown. The attacker makes sure to extend his right leg (on the mat) straight so that the defender's head is placed on the attacker's extended right leg.

The attacker uses his left hand to grab and control his opponent's left arm, pulling it. As he does this, the attacker places the top of his left foot on the back of his right knee (that is lying on the mat) to form the triangle with his legs. The attacker applies pressure with his legs and gets the tap out.

#2 Foot Wedge Against Opponent Who Is Balled Up in a Defensive Position

Sometimes the defender (the bottom grappler) will ball or curl up (as shown in this photo) in an effort to defend himself from his opponent. If the attacker wants to start a triangle choke from the front position, he can use his right foot and right leg to break open the bottom grappler's balled-up defensive position.

The attacker uses his right foot to jam or wedge in between the bottom grappler's left thigh and left arm or ribcage.

The attacker drives his right foot in hard between the bottom grappler's left upper leg and his ribcage.

After wedging his right foot and leg between the defender's left leg and left rib area, the attacker can immediately continue to roll to his right side and apply the triangle choke as shown in the previous series of photographs.

#3 Front Attack on Opponent Who Is on All Fours (in a No-Gi Situation)

The top grappler is positioned in front of the defender as shown.

The attacker uses his right arm to hook under the bottom grappler's left arm as shown.

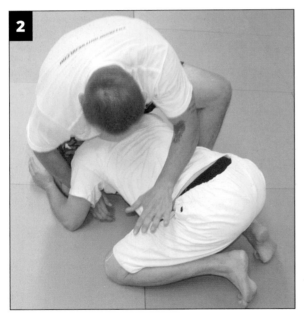

The attacker closes the space between his body and his opponent's body.

This photo shows how the attacker places his right upper leg directly at the bottom grappler's left shoulder. Doing this closes the space between the attacker and defender.

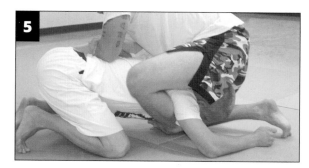

The attacker jams his left foot under the bottom grappler's right armpit. Doing this traps the bottom grappler's right arm and shoulder.

The attacker grasps his arms together, making sure to control the bottom grappler's left arm. As he does this, the top grappler uses his left leg to firmly hook and control the bottom grappler's right arm and shoulder.

The attacker rolls to his left side. Doing this forces the bottom grappler to roll onto his back as shown.

The attacker lies on his left side with the defender on his back as shown. The attacker forms the triangle with his feet and legs and uses his left arm to trap the defender's left arm.

#4 Double Trouble Bent Armlock

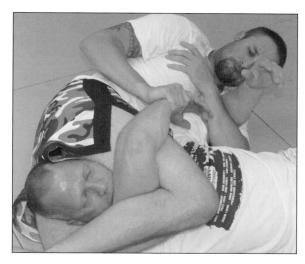

To make matters worse for the bottom grappler, the top grappler puts him in a double trouble situation and applies a bent armlock as he applies the triangle choke. The attacker uses his right hand to grab the defender's right wrist and cranks it forward and in the direction of the defender's stomach. This creates an effective bent armlock.

#5 Double Trouble Wrist Lock

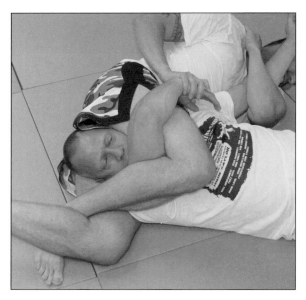

The attacker can also apply a strong wristlock (depending on what the rules of the sport allow) as he applies the triangle choke, putting the bottom fighter in a double trouble situation. The attacker uses his right hand to grab his opponent's right upper hand and bends it forward, forcing the defender's fingers in and downward. Doing this creates a good wristlock.

#6 Triangle Choke to North-South Pin

The attacker controls his opponent with a triangle as shown.

The attacker chooses to switch from his initial triangle control position.

The attacker shifts his body so that he sits on his buttocks. As he does this, the attacker uses his right hand and arm to hook under the defender's left arm for control.

The attacker uses his left hand (not shown) to grab under the body of the bottom grappler. The attacker uses his right hand to grab over and control the right upper body of the bottom man as shown.

The attacker quickly shifts his body and turns over onto the bottom grappler as shown.

The attacker kicks his right leg over so that he is positioned as shown.

The attacker settles in for the pin and holds the defender on his back on the mat.

#7 Triangle Choke to Leg Control Triangle Pin

The attacker has control over his opponent with a triangle choke, but for any number of reasons, the attacker may choose to switch and control his opponent with a pin or hold-down. This series of photos starts with the attacker controlling his opponent with a triangle and switching to a pin.

The attacker controls his opponent with a triangle choke.

The attacker uses his right hand to reach between the bottom grappler's legs and grabs the bottom grappler's left inner thigh. The attacker turns so that his chest is now facing the mat.

This photo shows how the attacker uses his right hand and arm to grab the defender's left upper leg for control. The attacker is turned so that he is belly down to the mat and pinning the bottom grappler.

This view shows how the attacker has maintained the triangle control with his legs and applies pressure to secure the choke. The defender's head is also trapped, and the triangle also produces a strong neck lock along with the choke.

#8 Snap Down to Triangle Choke

An effective way for the attacker to get his opponent down onto the mat is to snap him down. This photo shows the grapplers on their knees in a neutral position.

The attacker (left) uses his right hand to push down on the back of his opponent's head and neck as shown. This is the "snap down" that gets the defender onto his elbows and knees.

The top grappler uses his right foot and leg to hook over the bottom grappler's left armpit as shown. The attacker also jams his left upper leg against the bottom grappler's right shoulder to close the space between their two bodies.

The attacker rolls to his right and rolls the bottom grappler over as well.

The attacker rolls his opponent over onto his back as shown. The attacker forms a triangle with his feet and legs.

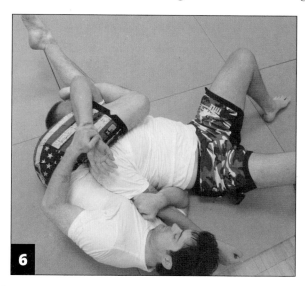

The attacker uses his left hand to grab and pull the bottom grappler's left hand. Doing this helps tighten the triangle. The attacker applies pressure with his legs and gets the tap out.

#9 Triangle Choke to Bent Armlock on Defender's Bottom Arm

The attacker controls his opponent with a triangle as shown.

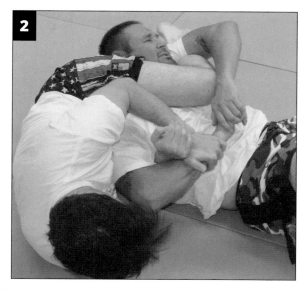

The top grappler uses his left hand to grab the right wrist of the defender. As he does this, the top grappler forms a keylock hold by using his right hand to grab his left wrist as shown.

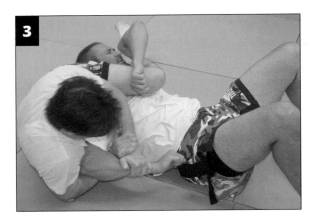

The top grappler now has a strong keylock and props up on his right elbow as shown. Doing this forces the defender's bent right arm so that it is elevated off of the mat. Doing this allows the attacker to more easily control the defender's bent right arm and allows the attacker to better apply the bent armlock from this position.

The attacker turns to his left so that he is face down on the mat. Doing this rotates his body and cranks the defender's bent right arm downward, creating pain. The attacker continues to use his legs formed in a triangle to apply pressure to choke his opponent. This creates "double trouble" with both a triangle choke and a bent armlock.

#10 Foot Prop Attack on Opponent Who Is Balled Up Tight

Sometimes the defender is balled up tight as shown.

The attacker places his right foot on the outside of the defender's left leg as shown.

The attacker pulls the defender over and uses his right foot and leg to prop or block the defender's left leg. Doing this forces the defender to roll over as shown.

The attacker rolls onto his right side as shown.

The attacker forms the triangle with his legs as he uses his hands and arms to control his opponent's arms.

This photo shows the finish position.

#11 Foot Prop Attack on Opponent Who Is Lying Flat on His Front

If the defender is foolish enough to lie flat on his front as shown in this photo he deserves what he gets.

The attacker uses his right foot to drive under the left armpit of the bottom grappler.

The attacker rolls to his right as shown.

The attacker pulls the defender over onto his back.

The attacker quickly forms the triangle with his legs.

The attacker uses his right hand to trap the defender's right wrist and hand. The attacker uses his left hand to grab the defender's jacket apron as shown.

The attacker forms a strong tie-up with the defender's jacket apron in a judo keylock as the attacker applies the triangle choke.

#12 Cradle Roll to Triangle Choke

The top grappler is standing and controls his opponent who is on all fours.

The top grappler steps in with his left foot and hooks his left leg over the bottom grappler's right shoulder.

The top grappler leans forward and starts to form a triangle with his legs as shown.

The top grappler forms a triangle with his feet and legs and traps the bottom grappler's head, left shoulder, and left arm. Look how far forward the top grappler leans over the bottom grappler.

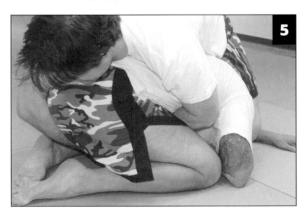

The top grappler uses his hands and arms to reach through the bottom grappler's right hip and leg. The top grappler grasps his hands together in a firm grip. Doing this starts the cradle move.

The top grappler has formed a strong triangle with his feet and legs and uses his hands and arms to form a cradle, trapping the bottom grappler's right hip and leg. The top grappler rolls to his left as shown.

This photo shows the attacker rolling to his left and rolling his opponent as well.

The attacker rolls his opponent over onto his back and applies pressure with his legs to secure the choke.

#13 Barrel Roll to Triangle Choke

The top grappler controls his opponent from the top.

The top grappler uses his right foot and leg to hook over and control the bottom grappler's left shoulder and arm.

The top grappler leans forward and onto his opponent's back.

The top grappler uses both hands and arms to reach around his opponent's body and grabs the bottom grappler's body. As he does this, the top grappler rolls to his right and rolls his opponent over with him.

The attacker rolls to his right side and rolls his opponent over onto his back. The attacker forms a triangle with his feet and legs.

The attacker uses his right hand and arm to trap his opponent's right arm. The attacker uses his left hand to grab and pull his opponent's left arm to tighten the triangle choke.

#14 Odd Side Roll to Triangle Choke

The defender is on elbows and knees as shown.

The attacker closes the space between the two bodies and uses his feet and legs to control his opponent's upper body.

Instead of rolling to his right (the side that the attacker has hooked the defender's armpit), the attacker rolls to his left.

The attacker drives his head between the bottom grappler's right leg and right arm (in what is called a "hole") and rolls to his left.

As the attacker rolls to his left, he pulls the defender over.

The attacker rolls over and is positioned on his right side. As he does this, he rolls the defender over onto his back.

The attacker starts to apply the triangle choke from this position.

The attacker finishes the triangle choke and gets the tap out.

#15 Reverse Triangle Choke Against Flat Opponent

The top grappler jams his left upper leg against the bottom grappler's right shoulder. The top grappler uses his right foot and leg to hook over the bottom grappler's left shoulder and arm.

The attacker leans to his left and starts to form a triangle with his feet and legs.

The attacker forms a triangle with his feet and legs and traps the bottom grappler so that the bottom grappler is flattened out on his front.

To make the triangle tighter, the top grappler may use his right hand to grab his left foot and place it more securely in the back of his right knee as shown. Look at how tightly the top grappler's triangle is being applied.

The top grappler leans forward to apply pressure from his hips to secure the triangle choke and the tap out.

#16 Sit Back to Reverse Triangle Choke

The attacker jams her left foot at the top of the bottom grappler's left shoulder.

The top grappler turns to her, swings her right foot and leg over the bottom grappler's body, and places her right foot on the mat for stability.

The top grappler uses her right hand and arm to reach under the right arm of the bottom grappler. The top grappler will use her right hand to grab her left ankle.

The top grappler uses her right hand to grab her left ankle as shown. Look at how the top grappler's left ankle is positioned on the mat and located over the bottom grappler's left shoulder.

This photo shows how the top grappler uses her right hand to firmly grab her left ankle.

The top grappler rolls to her left side. If necessary, she can use her left hand to post onto the mat for stability as she rolls to her left. The top grappler wants to roll to her left backside and onto her buttocks.

Rolling to her left, the attacker rolls the bottom grappler onto his back. The top grappler maintains a firm grip with her right hand on her left ankle. As she rolls onto her left side, the attacker will also roll onto her buttocks as shown.

The attacker forms a tight triangle with her feet and legs and applies the choke from this position.

#17 Triangle Choke as a Counter to Front Double-Leg Takedown

Both grapplers are facing each other in a standing position.

The grappler on the right drops in and attacks with a front double-leg takedown. The grappler on the left sprawls back to defend against the takedown attempt.

As he sprawls back, the attacker will next jam his left upper leg against his opponent's right shoulder.

The attacker uses his right foot and leg to hook over his opponent's left shoulder and arm. The top grappler uses both hands to grab tightly around his opponent's body to control him.

The top grappler rolls to his left as shown.

As he rolls to his left, the top grappler starts to form a triangle with his feet and legs.

The top grappler may have to use his right hand to grab his left ankle or foot to help pull it in tighter to form the triangle.

The attacker swings his right leg up and over to start to form the triangle.

The attacker forms the triangle with his feet and legs and continues to use his right hand to pull his left foot in tight and under his right knee to fully form the triangle.

The attacker has a tightly formed triangle with his feet and legs and uses both hands to hug his opponent's body for control. As he does this, the attacker applies pressure with his legs to secure the tap out.

#18 Foot Block and Triangle Choke Counter to Dougle-Leg Takedown

The attacker with his back to the camera shoots in for a double-leg takedown.

The grappler on the left anticipates the front takedown attempt and jams his left foot on his opponent's left hip as shown.

The grappler on the left rolls onto his left side and lands on the mat as shown. It appears as though the attacker has scored a takedown.

The grappler on the bottom (now the attacker) rolls onto his left side and swings his right foot and leg up and over his opponent's left arm and shoulder.

The attacker uses his right leg to hook over his opponent's left armpit area. The attacker extends his left leg out straight.

The attacker forms a triangle with his left foot placed behind his right knee. This is an unusual angle for a triangle but is a tight one.

The attacker applies pressure to the triangle with his legs, trapping his opponent in this position.

The attacker uses both hands and arms to reach around his opponent's body and grabs his hands together, forming a tight bear hug. As he does this, the attacker applies pressure with his legs and secures the triangle choke.

#19 Attacker Pulls Opponent Down to Triangle Choke from Neutral Position

The attacker (left) uses his right hand to hook behind his opponent's head as the attacker ducks under his opponent's right arm. The attacker uses his left hand to grab and control his opponent's right shoulder.

The attacker starts to drop under his opponent.

The attacker drops under his opponent and pulls him forward and down to the mat.

The attacker rolls onto his back and swings his right foot and leg up and over his opponent's left shoulder.

The attacker forms a triangle with his right foot placed in the back of his left knee. This starts a tight triangle hold.

The attacker secures the triangle hold as he continues to roll onto his back.

The attacker cinches in the triangle choke and gets the tap out.

This photo shows a front view of this tight triangle choke. The attacker continues to use his right hand to hook behind his opponent's head to help add more pressure to the triangle choke.

#20 Swing Under Triangle Choke Against a Kneeling Opponent

The attacker (left) stands. The defender is positioned on both knees. The attacker uses his right hand to grab over his opponent's left shoulder. The attacker uses his left hand and arm to hook under his opponent's right armpit.

The attacker makes sure to move to his opponent's front right corner as shown.

The attacker starts to swing his right foot and leg up as shown.

The attacker swings his body to his right and toward his kneeling opponent's left side.

The attacker swings his right foot and leg up and over his opponent's left shoulder.

The attacker swings under his opponent and uses his hands and arms to pull the defender forward. As he does this, the attacker starts to form the triangle with his feet and legs.

The attacker continues to swing to his right (and toward the defender's left side). As he does this, the attacker uses his left hand and arm to reach under his opponent's left leg for control. The attacker has a well-formed triangle at this point.

The attacker forms the triangle tightly as he continues to move to his right and at an angle under his opponent as shown.

The attacker rolls his opponent over as shown. Look at how the attacker uses his right hand and arm to control his opponent's left leg. Look at how the attacker uses his left hand to trap his opponent's right arm.

The attacker finishes the triangle choke in this position and gets the tap out.

TECHNICAL TIP: It's a bold move when a grappler or fighter jumps up and attempts a triangle choke on an opponent. Not only is it a bold move, it's a risky move; but with a lot of practice (and even more confidence), it can take an opponent by surprise. From a technical point of view, there are basically two applications that are most commonly used. The first is the "jump and roll" application where the attacker jumps up onto his opponent and uses the weight of his body and the momentum created by it as he jumps to roll the defender down and onto the mat, rolling him into a triangle choke. In this application, the attacker appears to jump past his opponent from a side or corner angle, and as the attacker forms the triangle with his legs, he falls to the mat and rolls his opponent over with him. The second application is the "jump and trap" where the attacker makes a more frontal assault and jumps directly up on his opponent, forms a triangle with his feet and legs around the defender's head and upper body, and then falls directly backward onto his own back, bringing the defender forward directly and ultimately into the triangle choke. These two primary applications of a jumping triangle choke are presented next.

#21 Jump and Roll Triangle Choke Against a Standing Opponent

The attacker (left) grips his opponent and positions his body so that he is at the defender's front right side.

The attacker starts to swing his right foot and leg up.

The attacker jumps up and swings his right foot and leg over the defender's left shoulder.

The attacker continues to hook his right foot and leg over his opponent's shoulder, head, and neck as the attacker continues to swing to his right and under his opponent.

The weight of the attacker's body starts to pull the defender forward.

The attacker continues to swing under his opponent and starts to form the triangle as shown.

The attacker places his right foot behind his left knee as he continues to swing under his opponent and pulls the defender forward and down to the mat.

The momentum of the attacker's body pulls the defender forward and down. The attacker continues to form the triangle with his feet and legs.

The attacker finishes the move as shown, placing his opponent in double trouble with a triangle choke and armlock.

#22 Jump and Trap Triangle Choke Against a Standing Opponent

This application of a jumping triangle is started with the attacker (left) positioned directly in front of his opponent.

This photo shows how the attacker is positioned directly in front of his opponent as the attacker jumps up.

The attacker quickly jumps up and swings his right foot and leg up and over the defender's left shoulder.

The attacker quickly uses his left hand to reach out and grab his right foot to help form the triangle more tightly.

The attacker may have to use both hands to grab his right lower leg or ankle to help form the triangle.

The attacker forms the triangle as shown. The pressure of the triangle choke may be enough to get the tap out at this point.

The attacker may fall onto his back and directly in front of (and under) the defender as he cinches in the triangle choke to get the tap out.

#23 Front Attack to a Triangle Pin

In some cases, the attacker may choose to use a pin or hold-down rather than a triangle choke. This series of photos shows such a situation.

The attacker approaches his opponent from the front as shown.

The attacker rolls to his right in a standard front approach to the triangle choke.

The attacker rolls his opponent over and onto his back.

The attacker forms a strong triangle with his feet and legs.

To secure the pin, the attacker turns over onto his front and uses his left hand and arm to reach forward and grab the defender's right lower leg.

The attacker uses his left hand and arm to reach around and grab the defender's lower leg or ankle. This secures the pin.

#24 Upside-Down Triangle Pin

The attacker approaches his opponent from the front as shown.

The attacker uses the standard setup to start the triangle choke from this front position.

The attacker rolls to his right side and pulls his opponent over as shown.

The attacker rolls onto his right side and starts to secure the triangle from this position.

The attacker starts to form the triangle with his feet and legs.

As he secures his triangle with his feet and legs, the attacker starts to turn his body to his right and uses his right hand and arm (not shown) to push off the mat.

The attacker rolls over onto his front and uses his left hand to grab his opponent's midsection or belt for control. The attacker continues to use his leg triangle to control his opponent in this pin.

#25 Upside Down Reverse Triangle Choke

This application is also called the "belly up" triangle choke or the "north south" triangle choke.

The attacker starts from a position where he kneels at the bottom grappler's right shoulder area.

The attacker moves his right foot and leg over his opponent's head and over the bottom man's left shoulder. Look at the angle the attacker has as he does this.

The attacker rolls onto his right side and slides his right foot and leg over the bottom grappler's left shoulder. The attacker places his right foot behind his left knee. The attacker may be able to tighten his legs to secure the triangle choke from this position, but if that is not possible, the attacker will continue.

The attacker rolls to his right and onto his back. As he does this, the attacker forces the defender to roll over as well.

The attacker finishes the choke from this position.

#26 Attacker Rolls Over Defender's Back as Defender Sits Up

The top grappler attacks his opponent from the front as shown.

The bottom grappler attempts to defend against the triangle choke by sitting up as shown. As the defender does this, the attacker uses both hands and arms to grab around the defender's body.

The attacker forms a triangle with his feet and legs as shown.

As the defender continues to rise, the attacker rolls over to his right with the defender in a tight triangle hold. Look at how the attacker uses his hands and arms to grab around and control the defender's body.

The attacker rolls over his right shoulder and right side.

As the attacker rolls, he maintains the triangle hold with his feet and legs and his body lock with his hands and arms. Doing this rolls the defender over.

The attacker rolls over onto his left side as shown and rolls the defender over onto his back.

The attacker finishes the move by tightening the triangle with his legs to secure the tap out.

#27 Head-Only Triangle from Front Attack

The top grappler attacks his opponent from the front position.

The attacker places his left foot on the mat at the bottom grappler's right elbow as shown.

The attacker rolls to his left side and forces his opponent over with him.

The attacker positions his feet and legs so that only the defender's head is trapped in the triangle.

The attacker is positioned on his left side and forms a triangle around the head of his opponent.

The attacker turns over onto his front as shown. Doing this starts the strangling process of the triangle hold.

As the attacker turns onto his front, he cinches the triangle hold tighter. Doing this creates both a nasty choke and a strong neck crank.

The attacker may move his head and body more to his left and create an even stronger choke.

#28 Head-Only Leg Grab Triangle

The attacker (left) approaches his opponent from the front as shown.

The attacker places his right foot and leg on the outside of the bottom grappler's left arm.

The attacker rolls to his right side and forces his opponent over onto his back.

This photo from another view shows how the attacker is positioned on his left side and how he moves his left leg up and over the bottom grappler's head.

The attacker forms a tight triangle hold on the defender's head. Look at how the attacker uses his hands and arms to trap the defender's right arm.

The attacker uses his left hand to reach over and grab the defender's right leg.

The attacker turns to his left (and into the defender) and uses his left hand and arm to hook and grab the defender's right leg. Doing this creates a strong triangle choke and neck lock on the defender's head.

Attacking an opponent from a front ride or neutral position is a favorite among many good grapplers and fighters. It's a good idea for every grappler to have more than one effective setup from a front ride or front neutral position.

In the next chapter, triangle chokes starting from a back ride position will be presented. Getting an opponent's back and controlling him is a strong starting position, and there are many interesting things that contribute to the success of triangle chokes started from this position, so let's get started.

Part 4: Triangles

From the Back Ride Position

"GET HIS BACK"

These three words say a lot to those of us in the world of fighting sports. Getting behind an opponent and taking his back is a fundamental skill that sets up a variety of submission techniques and finishing moves.

"Getting his back" is what takes place when a grappler is able to control the position so that he is behind his opponent. From there, the attacker works to control his opponent from this rear position so he can control his opponent's movement in order to work into a choke, armlock, leglock, pin, or other finishing technique. In MMA or in a self-defense situation, strikes and other methods of finishing the fight can also be employed.

How the attacker controls his opponent from the back depends on what the attacker ultimately wants to do. For instance, in amateur folkstyle wrestling, getting behind an opponent and riding him can earn points for the wrestler who controls the ride. In submission grappling, catch wrestling, MMA, sambo, BJJ, or judo, points aren't scored for riding an opponent for time from behind. The primary goal when riding an opponent is to secure a submission technique. So, tactically, getting behind an opponent and controlling the position with a ride has the ultimate goal of making the opponent tap out or submit. Further, how the attacker controls his opponent with a ride from the back often depends on what submission technique he wants to attack with.

This chapter presents some triangle chokes that can be applied when the attacker is behind his opponent and has his back. Tactically, the attacker who controls his opponent from the back wants to control the movement of his opponent with a ride but must make sure to be mobile enough in his ride so his feet and legs can be used as weapons and form a triangle in order to further control his opponent and secure the triangle choke to get a tap out. In other words, if the goal for the attacker is to get a triangle choke, he should make sure to have his feet and legs free enough so he has the freedom of movement and mobility to work in and form a triangle with his feet and legs.

RIDE TO CONTROL AN OPPONENT

A "ride" is a term used in a variety of combat sports to denote control. A ride is a temporary position that the attacker uses to maintain control of his opponent for as long as necessary to secure a finishing hold or submission technique or to go on to another position of control. The ability to control an opponent with a ride is a skill that every grappler or fighter should spend a considerable amount of time working on. Any grappler or fighter who wants to finish the match or fight and get a submission (for the purposes of our discussion, a triangle choke) must control the position first. As I've written in a number of my books, "Control the position and get the submission." For a comprehensive examination of rides that are useful in jujitsu, submission grappling, MMA, and catch wrestling, I recommend the book I coauthored with John Saylor, *Vital Jujitsu* (to get a copy, you can email me at stevescottjudo@yahoo.com).

While there are quite a few riding and controlling positions from the back, for the purposes of securing a triangle choke when behind an opponent, this chapter will focus on three primary rides. They are:

(1) The Rodeo Ride. This is also called the "rear mount," "back ride," or "getting the hooks in." I first heard the term "rodeo ride" used by John Saylor at the U.S. Olympic Training Center about 1984. It explains this controlling position quite well. John coined this name because, as he put it, "It looks like the top fighter is riding a bull in the rodeo." The ideal situation is for the top grappler to control his opponent by "getting the opponent's back" and "getting his hooks in" and controlling the bottom grappler with both leg control and hand/arm control. The major distinguishing feature of any rodeo ride is that the top grappler's hips and midline of his body have contact with his opponent's hips and midline of the defender's body. Another distinguishing feature of this ride is that the top grappler often has one or both legs hooked into the hip or hips (or leg or legs) of the bottom grappler. Because of this, the attacker must ensure that he can get one or both of his legs free in order to use them to secure a triangle

position. This is a consideration when a grappler controls his opponent with a rodeo ride. If he wants to work in a triangle, the controlling grappler must be able to have the freedom of movement with his feet and legs so that he can use them to triangle his opponent.

(2) The Seated Rodeo Ride. In this ride, the attacker is seated on his buttocks behind the defender. This is a variation of the rodeo ride and is used often in just about every fighting sport. As in the basic approach to the rodeo ride, the ideal position for the attacker is to maintain control of his opponent from behind using both his legs and his hands and arms. As with the rodeo ride, the attacker must make sure to use the seated rodeo ride so he has enough freedom of movement with his feet and legs to secure a triangle choke.

(3) The Standing or Squatting Ride. In this ride, the top grappler is either standing or squatting behind his opponent (who may be on all fours or lying flat on his front). This may look like a rodeo ride without the top grappler using his foot or leg to control the bottom grappler's lower body. To the untrained eye, this ride may not appear to afford the top (attacking) grappler enough control over his opponent. However, this is a strong controlling ride and allows the attacker the full use of his lower extremities by not having one (or both) legs hooked into the defender's hips. This mobility of the feet and legs is often ideal for setting up the defender for a triangle choke. Often, this ride is the ride that a triangle choke specialist will focus on to control his opponent from a back ride position.

FUNCTIONAL APPLICATIONS USING THE THREE PRIMARY RIDES

RODEO RIDE

The top grappler is positioned on his opponent's back, with the attacker often using his feet and legs to control his opponent's lower body and hips and using his hands and arms to control his opponent's upper body. This sequence of photos presents a frequently used triangle choke when the attacker "has his opponent's back" and "has his hooks in."

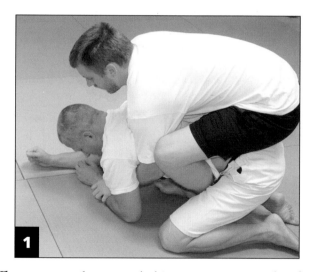

The top grappler controls his opponent using his feet and legs to control the bottom grappler's hips and lower body. The top grappler uses his hands and arms to control the bottom man's upper body.

The top grappler moves his right foot and leg over his opponent's right shoulder as the top grappler rolls to his right. As he does this, the top grappler uses his left hand to grab his right ankle to start to form the triangle with his legs.

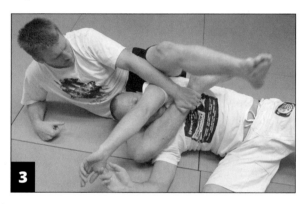

The top grappler rolls to his right and forces the bottom grappler to roll as well. Look at how the top grappler uses his left hand to pull his right lower leg (his anchor leg) in and under his left knee.

The top grappler forms the triangle with his feet and legs to finish the sequence.

SEATED RODEO RIDE

The key feature of the seated rodeo ride is that both the attacker and defender are seated on their buttocks on the mat as shown in this sequence of photos with the attacker usually using his feet and legs to control his opponent's lower body. The attacker also often uses his hands and arms to control his opponent's upper body. This ride provides a strong and stable base to initiate a triangle choke.

The attacker is seated on his buttocks behind the defender. The defender uses his feet and legs to control his opponent's hips and lower body and uses his hands and arms to control the defender's upper body.

The attacker shifts his grip with his hand and arms and prepares to change his position to start his triangle choke.

3

The attacker shifts the position of his body so that he has the freedom of movement to start to move his left foot and leg up and over the defender's left arm and shoulder to start to form the triangle.

4

The attacker forms the triangle with his feet and legs to finish the move.

STANDING RIDE

The standing ride and its many variations have a great many uses in every fighting sport. The most recognizable feature of the standing (or squatting) ride is that the attacker's base is on his feet and not on his knees or buttocks. Also, the attacker often does not use his feet or legs to hook or entwine the defender's leg or legs. Doing this allows for a greater range of movement and mobility for the attacker, allowing him to use his feet and legs more freely when attacking with a triangle choke.

This sequence of photos shows one of many ways the attacker can start a triangle choke from a standing or squatting ride.

1

The top grappler controls his opponent with a standing ride using a wide base for stability.

2

The top grappler moves his left foot and leg over his opponent's head to start to form the triangle.

3

The attacker continues to drive his left foot and leg over the bottom grappler's right shoulder and under his left armpit as shown. The top grappler posts on the top of his head on the mat for stability.

The top grappler forms the triangle with his feet and legs to secure the triangle choke from this position.

> **TECHNICAL TIP:** These three rides (and variations of them) will be used in this chapter to break the opponent down to secure triangle chokes. As stated before, there are a variety of rides and controlling positions from behind an opponent, so take what is presented here and expand on it so that it works for you.

BODY TRIANGLES WHEN THE ATTACKER HAS HIS OPPONENT'S BACK

Another way to apply a triangle when behind an opponent is to use the body triangle. A body triangle is done when the attacker forms a triangle with his legs around the trunk of his opponent's body. Some combat sports (such as judo) may not allow the attacker to apply a body triangle with the intent of applying pressure with the legs to constrict the defender's torso or body. (This is called "dojime" or "body constriction or squeezing," as mentioned previously.) However, many combat sports have no rule against the use of body triangles, and they are a viable weapon in the arsenal of every grappler or fighter.

BODY TRIANGLE FROM A RODEO RIDE

In some situations, the top grappler can apply a body triangle from a rodeo ride position as shown in this photo. This affords the top grappler a great deal of control over his opponent, and this control gives the attacker more time to work in a submission technique (such as a rear naked choke) or punish the defender with punches if in a fight or MMA match. The attacker can also use the body triangle from this rodeo ride to constrict or squeeze his opponent's torso to force the defender to tap out from the pressure of the body triangle.

BODY TRIANGLE FROM A SEATED RODEO RIDE

The attacker may have initially applied his body triangle on his opponent from a rodeo ride and rolled the defender over onto his buttocks as shown in this photo. In any event, this ride provides a strong base for the attacker, who is positioned behind the defender. By using a body triangle the attacker (from behind) has excellent control of his opponent and can apply a submission technique from this position or use the body triangle to squeeze and constrict his opponent's torso to cause pain.

BODY SCISSORS FROM A RODEO RIDE

Another method for the attacker to use his legs to constrict his opponent is to use a body scissors from a back ride or rodeo ride position. Body scissors were examined in the first chapter on the core skills in the introduction and have been used in catch wrestling and submission grappling for many years. The primary purpose of the body scissors is to

apply pressure to the defender's torso, but a good secondary purpose is to provide control for the attacker so he can secure another finishing hold or submission technique.

With these fundamental factors in mind, let's continue on to some practical ways of applying triangle chokes when positioned behind an opponent.

#1 Ankle Grab Roll to Triangle Choke

The top grappler controls his opponent with a rodeo ride.

The top grappler moves his right foot and leg over the right shoulder of the bottom grappler.

The top grappler uses his left hand to grab the ankle or low on his right leg.

The top grappler starts to roll forward and over his right shoulder as he pulls on his right ankle with his left hand.

The top grappler rolls over his right shoulder and side as shown.

As he rolls to his right, the top grappler uses his left hand to pull his right ankle and foot in tightly over the bottom grappler's right shoulder as shown. As he does this, the top grappler moves his left foot and leg over the left side of the defender's body.

The attacker uses his left hand to pull his right ankle and foot in tightly under his left knee as shown. This starts to form a tight triangle.

The attacker cinches in tightly with his feet and legs to form a tight triangle.

To add more pressure to the triangle, the top grappler can use his left hand to grab and pull his left ankle as shown.

As a method to get his opponent into double trouble, the attacker uses both of his hands and arms to grab and pull the defender's left arm up and in the direction of the attacker's head.

The attacker uses both hands and arms to trap and hook the defender's extended left arm. Doing this puts the defender in double trouble with both a nasty triangle choke and an armlock.

To add more pressure to the armlock, the attacker can use his right hand to grab his shoulder. Doing this traps the defender's extended left arm as shown. As he does this, the attacker can use his left hand to grab and pull his left ankle to cinch the triangle choke in tighter.

#2 Belly-Down Triangle from Back Ride

The top grappler controls the bottom grappler with a rodeo ride without getting his legs hooked in as shown.

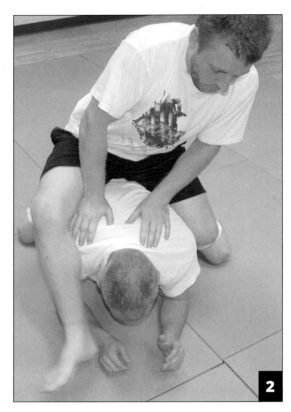

The top grappler places his right foot and leg over the bottom grappler's right shoulder.

The top grappler digs his right foot and leg in over the bottom man's right shoulder, making sure to hook it in tightly.

The top grappler uses his left hand to grab his right ankle and pulls his right ankle in tightly.

This photo shows the top grappler using his left hand to reach under the bottom man's left arm and grab his right ankle and pull in across the bottom grappler's chest.

TECHNICAL TIP: The top grappler should make sure to use his left hand to grab and pull his right foot (his anchor foot) so that it firmly traps and controls the bottom grappler's upper body.

The top grappler moves his left foot and leg so that the top of his right foot is placed on the back of his left knee as shown. Doing this firmly traps the bottom grappler in a tight triangle.

The top grappler drives his hips down and forward. Doing this stretches the bottom grappler out flat and secures the tap out from the triangle choke.

#3 Arm Drag Belly-Down Triangle Choke

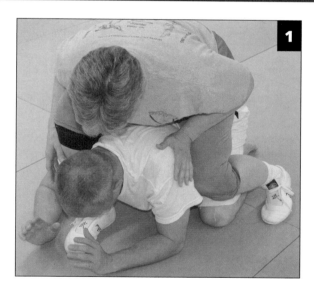

This is a similar move to #2, but the top grappler will pull the bottom grappler's arm out, stretching and extending it to secure the choke. The top grappler controls her opponent with a top ride as shown.

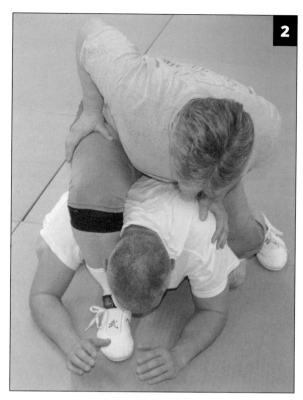

The top grappler moves her right foot and leg over the bottom grappler's right shoulder.

The top grappler uses his right hand to grab the bottom grappler's left wrist.

The top grappler uses his right hand to pull the bottom grappler's left wrist, extending his arm out straight.

The top grappler jams her right foot and leg in over the bottom grappler's right shoulder, trapping it. As she does this, the top grappler starts to roll to her right.

The top grappler slides her left foot over so that the top of her right foot is placed in the back of her left leg. As she does this, the top grappler continues to roll to her right so that she is positioned on her right hip for stability. Rolling to her right gives the top grappler the necessary room to secure her triangle.

The top grappler uses both hands to grab the bottom grappler's extended left arm and pulls it. Doing this allows the top grappler to firmly secure the triangle that has been formed with her legs and make it tighter.

The top grappler drives her hips downward and onto the back of the bottom grappler as she tightens the triangle with her legs to apply pressure and secure the tap out.

#4 Side Roll Triangle Choke from Standing Ride

The top grappler controls the bottom grappler. As she does this, the top grappler uses her left hand to grab the bottom grappler's right lapel.

The top grappler moves her right foot and leg over the right shoulder of the bottom grappler.

This front view shows how the top grappler uses her left hand to grab her opponent's right lapel and uses her right foot and leg that are positioned over the bottom grappler's right shoulder. This is a tight strangle from this position, but the top grappler will make it even worse for the bottom grappler.

The top grappler rolls to her left side onto her buttocks.

The top grappler uses her right foot to hook behind the back of her left leg. (As the attacker does not have long legs, she places the top of her right foot behind her left calf muscle.) The attacker continues to use her right hand to grab and control the defender's left wrist.

As the top grappler rolls to her right, she uses her right hand to grab and pull her opponent's left arm, extending it. Doing this helps the attacker cinch her right foot and leg in tighter across her opponent's chest.

The attacker uses her right hand to reach for the bottom grappler's left hand.

The attacker forms a tight triangle for the choke and uses her left hand to grab and control the bottom grappler's bent left arm. The attacker uses her right hand to push the defender's left wrist and creates a bent armlock to secure both a triangle choke and bent armlock for double trouble and a sure tap out.

The attacker uses her left hand to pull the bottom grappler's left hand upward so that she can use her left foot and leg to drive under the bottom grappler's left shoulder.

#5 Body Triangle to Hadaka Jime (Naked Choke)

The top grappler uses his left foot and leg to hook and control the bottom grappler's midsection. Look at how the top grappler uses his left foot to wedge and "anchor" onto the bottom man's right hip for control.

The top grappler moves his right foot and leg forward and forms a triangle by placing the top of his left foot in the back of his right knee as shown.

This forms a tight body triangle. The top grappler can squeeze his legs tightly and force the bottom grappler to tap out from the pressure of the body triangle at this point.

The top grappler rolls to his left over his shoulder. Doing this forces the bottom grappler to roll also.

The top grappler rolls to his left and rolls his opponent over with him; all the while the top grappler maintains firm control with the body triangle as shown. Look at how the top grappler uses his left hand to grab and control the defender's left wrist.

The top grappler uses his right hand to reach around his opponent's head and neck as the top grappler maintains control with his left hand on his opponent's left wrist.

The attacker can apply a great deal of pressure with his body triangle from this position and force his opponent to tap out.

The attacker can also apply a strong figure four rear naked choke from this position.

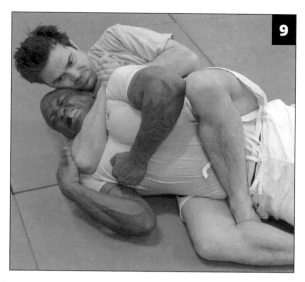

The attacker can also apply a nasty square-grip-style rear naked choke from this position to get the tap out as well.

#6 Step-Over Triangle from Side Ride

The top grappler rides his opponent from the side as shown. This is also a good transition from a throw or takedown to a triangle choke.

The top grappler drives his right foot and leg over the top of the bottom grappler's head.

The top grappler slides his right foot over the bottom grappler's left shoulder and places the top of his right foot on the back of his left knee. This forms the triangle. As he does this, the top grappler rolls over his right shoulder.

The top grappler rolls over to his right side and uses his hands and arms to grab his opponent's near (right) leg for stability. As he does this, the attacker squeezes his triangle tight to get the tap out.

#7 Head Roll Triangle Choke

The top grappler rides his opponent with a standing ride from the side as shown.

The top grappler moves his left foot and leg over the top of the bottom grappler's head as the top grappler leans forward.

The top grappler places the top of his right foot on the back of the bottom grappler as the top grappler uses his hands and arms to form a keylock to control the bottom grappler's right arm.

The top grappler rolls over his right shoulder.

The top grappler threads his left foot under the left armpit of the defender as shown.

This photo shows how the attacker controls the bottom grappler with his hands and arms as well as his left foot and leg. The top grappler posts on the top of his head at this point.

This top view shows the position of the attacker's body in relation to the position of the defender's body.

The attacker extends his right leg out straight over the back of the bottom grappler.

The attacker forms the triangle by placing the top of his left foot on the inside of his right knee. This is a tight triangle from this position.

The top grappler rolls to his left side. Doing this tightens the triangle and forces the bottom grappler to start to roll over his head.

The attacker continues to roll over his left side, forcing his opponent to continue to roll over his head.

This photo shows the attacker rolling his opponent.

The attacker continues to roll, forcing his opponent to roll over as well.

The attacker completes the roll and rolls the defender flat onto his back as shown. Look at how the attacker maintains the keylock with his hands and arms and maintains the tight triangle with his feet and legs. The attacker is now lying on his left side.

This photo shows the position of the attacker in relation to the position of the defender.

The attacker finishes the move by moving over onto his front to secure a tight triangle choke, a tight pin, and a tight bent armlock.

#8 Head Roll Triangle Choke from a Juji Gatame Attempt

The attacker (top grappler) has positioned his body so that he can secure a juji gatame (cross-body armlock) from this top position. The bottom grappler may have pulled his arm back in and the top grappler now chooses to switch to a triangle choke.

The top grappler is positioned so that his left foot and leg are under the left side of his opponent's body. The top grappler is posted on the top of his head for stability.

The top grappler forms a triangle with his left foot in the back of his right knee as shown.

The top grappler cinches in the triangle he has formed with his left foot behind his right knee. The attacker can apply pressure with his legs to secure the triangle

choke from this position and get a tap out. But if this is not successful, the top grappler will roll his opponent over onto the opponent's back.

The top grappler rolls to his right and forces the bottom grappler to roll over in the direction of the bottom grappler's head.

The attacker rolls and forces the defender to also roll.

The attacker rolls his opponent over and onto his back. All the while, the attacker maintains control of the triangle with his feet and legs.

The attacker applies pressure with his legs to get the tap out from the triangle choke as he levers or loosens the defender's arms in order to secure the juji gatame armlock from this leg press position.

The attacker secures both the triangle choke and the armlock to get a tap out from this double trouble move.

#9 Head Sit Triangle Choke

The top grappler rides his opponent using his right hand to grab and control the bottom man's right arm. Look at how the top grappler uses his left hand to push down on the bottom grappler's head.

The top grappler moves his left foot and leg forward.

The top grappler slides his left foot and leg over the back of the bottom grappler's head and uses his left foot to dig deep under the right chest area of the bottom grappler.

The top grappler leans to his left as he uses his right hand to control his opponent's right wrist and forearm. Doing this forces the bottom grappler to lean forward.

The top grappler leans to his left side and forces his opponent to roll forward in a somersault.

The top grappler has rolled his opponent over and the attacker is lying on his left side.

As he finishes the roll, the top grappler uses his right hand to grab his left foot and pulls his left foot in tightly behind his right knee to start to form the triangle.

This closer view shows how the attacker uses his right hand to pull his foot in tightly behind his right knee to secure the triangle choke and get the tap out.

#10 Near Wrist Judo Keylock to Triangle Choke

The top grappler rides his opponent as shown. As he does this, the top grappler uses his right hand and arm to reach under the bottom grappler's right arm. The top grappler uses his right hand to grab and trap the bottom grappler's left wrist in a near wrist ride.

The top grappler firmly controls his opponent with the near wrist ride.

The top grappler quickly explodes up off the mat and moves to his right and around to the front of the bottom grappler.

The top grappler moves all the way around and to the front of his opponent. As he does this, the top grappler starts to tie up his opponent's right lower arm with a judo keylock.

The top grappler secures the judo keylock on his opponent's right arm.

The top grappler squats on his opponent in this head sit position and controls the bottom grappler with a strong judo keylock.

The top grappler rolls to his right side, forcing the bottom grappler to roll also.

The attacker rolls to his right side and secures the triangle choke from this position.

The attacker finishes the triangle choke with the judo keylock to get the tap out.

#11 Triangle Choke from a Standing Ride Against a Flat Opponent

The top grappler controls his opponent with a standing ride. The bottom grappler is lying flat on his front in a defensive position.

The top grappler uses his right hand to reach under the bottom grappler's right armpit area and start to grab the bottom man's right wrist.

The top grappler uses his right hand to control his opponent's right wrist, pulling it tightly to the bottom man's right chest area.

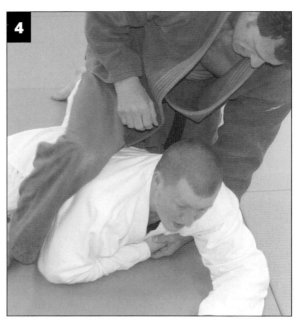

The top grappler reaches under the bottom grappler's left armpit and uses his left hand to grab and pull his opponent's right arm. As he does this, the top grappler starts to use his right foot and leg to step over his opponent's right arm.

The attacker uses his left hand to pull on the bottom grappler's right arm to trap it. Doing this allows the top grappler to more effectively move his right foot and leg over the bottom man's right shoulder.

The top grappler uses his left hand to grab his right ankle as shown to gain tight control over the bottom grappler.

The top grappler starts to roll forward to his right side. He may have to place his right hand or arm on the mat for stability.

The attacker rolls over onto his right hip and props his body up with his right arm as shown. As he does this, the attacker uses his left hand to grab his right ankle and slides it tightly under the neck of the defender.

The attacker swings his left foot and leg upward and uses his left hand to grab and pull his right ankle to place his right foot under and behind the back of his left knee.

The attacker forms the triangle.

The attacker finishes the move by using both hands and arms to grab and trap the defender's left arm to secure the juji gatame. As he does this, the attacker applies pressure with his legs to secure the triangle choke and get the tap out from this double trouble situation.

#12 Fake Armlock from Standing Ride to Triangle Choke

The top grappler stands above his opponent and uses his left hand and arm to grab and hook under the bottom grappler's left armpit area.

The attacker uses his left hand and arm to hook and pull his opponent's left arm up. Doing this often fools the bottom grappler into believing the top grappler is attempting an armlock from this position.

The attacker quickly uses his right foot and leg to step over the bottom grappler's right shoulder.

The attacker starts to roll forward over to his right as shown. He may have to place his right hand on the mat for stability as he starts his roll.

The attacker rolls to his right and as he rolls, he forces the bottom grappler to roll also.

The attacker finishes his roll and lands so that he is propped up on his right elbow as shown. As he does this, the attacker uses his left hand to grab and trap his opponent's left arm, and the attacker also forms a triangle with his feet and legs.

The attacker forms a tight triangle as shown as he stays positioned on his right side.

The attacker uses his left hand to hook and trap his opponent's left arm and uses his right hand to grab and pull the extended left arm to secure the armlock. As he does this, the attacker applies pressure with the triangle choke to get the tap out.

#13 Rolling Triangle Choke

The top grappler controls his opponent with a standing ride as shown. The attacker uses his left hand to grab the bottom grappler's right lapel tightly under the bottom grappler's chin.

The attacker uses his right foot and leg to step over the bottom grappler's body as shown.

The top grappler slides his right foot and leg over and "through the hole" between the bottom man's right arm and right knee. The top grappler uses his right hand to grab his opponent's right upper leg to help roll him over.

This shows how the attacker rolls directly over the side of his opponent and how the top grappler drives his head forcefully "though the hole" to make the bottom man roll over.

This photo shows the rolling action. Look at how the attacker uses his left hand to grab and pull his opponent's lapel tightly around his throat as he rolls.

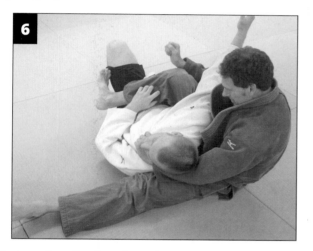

The attacker finishes the roll and swings his right foot and leg over his opponent's hip and torso area as he finishes the roll.

The attacker moves his right foot up so that it is placed near his left hand.

The attacker swings his left leg up and over his right foot to form the triangle. Look at how the attacker continues to choke his opponent with his left hand on the lapel of the jacket. The defender often taps out at this point.

If the defender does not tap out, the attacker forms a tight triangle with his feet and legs and uses both hands to grab and trap his opponent's right arm to secure a juji gatame armlock and apply pressure with the triangle choke to get the tap out.

#14 Step-Over Leg Choke Against Flat Opponent

The top grappler controls his opponent who is lying flat on his front in a defensive position.

The top grappler uses his left foot and leg to step over the bottom grappler's left shoulder. As he does this, the top grappler jams his left heel in tightly against the left side of the bottom grappler's neck.

The top grappler uses his right hand to grab his left ankle and pull it in tightly against the left side of the bottom grappler's neck. Doing this creates a strong choke.

If the bottom grappler is a tough guy and doesn't tap out from the standing leg choke, the top grappler leans forward and places his left hand on the mat for stability. As he does this, the top grappler continues to add pressure to the choke.

The top grappler leans forward and posts on the top of his head for stability. The momentum of the top grappler's body leaning forward and over the bottom grappler adds more pressure to the leg choke and gets the tap out.

#15 Necktie Leg Choke

The top grappler rides his opponent as shown.

The top grappler uses his right foot and leg to step over the bottom grappler's head. As he does this, the top grappler makes sure to pull his right foot in tightly against the far (left) side of the bottom grappler's head to trap it.

The top grappler quickly uses his right hand to reach under his opponent's head and neck and grabs his right

ankle. The top grappler pulls hard on his ankle. Doing this traps the bottom grappler's head between the top grappler's lower right leg and right arm.

#16 Seated Rodeo Ride to Triangle Choke from the Back

This is a popular and effective basic application of the triangle choke from a seated rodeo ride behind an opponent.

The attacker controls his opponent from behind in a seated rodeo ride using both hands to grab and control his opponent's left arm.

The attacker swings his left foot and leg up and over his opponent's left arm.

The attacker moves his left foot and leg over his opponent's left shoulder as shown. As he does this, the attacker rolls back slightly onto his lower back.

TECHNICAL TIP: The attacker who is behind his opponent in a seated rodeo ride should initially stay on his buttocks and not lie on his back or side. By lying on his back or side, the attacker bears the weight of the defender, and this will restrict the mobility and movement of the attacker.

The attacker moves his right foot and leg up and prepares to hook his right leg over his left foot to form the triangle.

The attacker forms the triangle with his feet and legs. After doing this, the attacker rolls to his left side to tighten the triangle.

The attacker quickly uses both hands to grab and trap his opponent's right arm to secure the juji gatame armlock and apply the triangle choke.

TECHNICAL TIP: The attacker stays on his left side as he finishes this technique. Doing this enables the attacker to arch his hips with more force, giving more strength to his legs in his triangle choke and more leverage in applying his juji gatame armlock.

#17 Seated Rodeo Ride Foot Prop to Triangle Choke

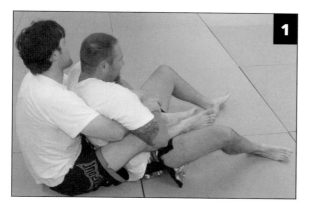

The attacker controls his opponent from behind with a seated rodeo ride.

The attacker places his right foot against his opponent's right hip and buttock and uses his right foot to push. Doing this creates some space as shown. The attacker has good control of his opponent's arms as shown.

The attacker uses his right foot to push back and move slightly to the left side of his opponent. Doing this gives the attacker room to move his right foot and leg up to form the triangle.

The attacker swings his right foot and leg up and over the defender's right shoulder. The attacker uses his left hand (that is positioned under the defender's left armpit) to grab his right ankle.

The attacker uses his left hand to grab and pull his right ankle and foot up and behind the back of his left knee to form a tight triangle. As he does this, the attacker rolls to his left hip to add pressure to the choke.

The attacker quickly uses both hands to grab and pull the left arm of the defender to secure a triangle choke and an armlock to put his opponent in double trouble and get the tap out.

#18 Seated Rodeo Ride to Leg Press Triangle Choke

The attacker controls his opponent from behind in a seated rodeo ride. Look at how the attacker uses both hands to grab and control his opponent's left wrist and arm.

The attacker moves his right hand and arm over the back of his opponent's head.

The attacker spins to his left side as he swings his right foot and leg over the head of his opponent.

The attacker maintains a strong keylock with his hands and arms to control his opponent's left arm. As he does this, the attacker moves his right foot back and starts to slide his left foot and leg over the chest of his opponent as shown.

The attacker starts to form the triangle with his feet and legs as shown.

The attacker forms the triangle from this side position and applies pressure to get the tap out.

TECHNICAL TIP: There will be more on applying triangle chokes from the leg press position in the next chapter.

Working a triangle choke on an opponent from a back ride position is an aggressive way to get a tap out. Some of the sneakiest (and remember, sneaky is good when it applies to chokes and strangles) setups used for triangle chokes start from when one grappler or fighter has his opponent's back. Don't hesitate to use what's been presented in this chapter and make it work for you.

Now let's turn our attention to securing triangle chokes when initially holding or pinning an opponent. In some fighting sports, holding an opponent for time may win the match, but that's not always the case, so let's look at how to finish an opponent with a triangle choke from a position of holding or pinning.

"Park him there until he quits."
Shawn Watson

Part 5: Triangle Chokes
When Controlling or Pinning an Opponent

APPLYING A TRIANGLE CHOKE AFTER CONTROLLING AN OPPONENT WITH A HOLD OR PIN

Shawn Watson's advice to "park him there until he quits" is based on the dual concept of (1) controlling an opponent with a pin or time hold, making it so miserable and painful and applying so much pressure from the hold that he taps out or (2) controlling an opponent with a pin or time hold to control an opponent long enough to allow ample time to secure a submission technique or finishing hold. In most forms of submission grappling and fighting (including sambo, freestyle judo, BJJ, and MMA), a fighter or grappler can't win by a pin or hold-down. He or she must use the pin or hold-down as a method to secure and control an opponent in order to either apply so much pressure with the hold-down that the opponent submits or, more often, use the hold-down or pin to control the opponent long enough to work in a submission technique.

This chapter of the book focuses on using a hold-down or pin as a controlling position in order to finish off an opponent with a triangle choke. The advice that I come back to time and again in this book is certainly true here as well: control the position and get the submission.

THE CONCEPT OF A "TIME HOLD"

In 1966, I read a book that changed my outlook on grappling. The book was *The Handbook of Judo* by Gene LeBell and Laurie Coughran. While there was a lot of great information in this book, one of the things that influenced me the most was the concept of a "time hold": not only making the hold or pin so miserable and painful that the guy on bottom wants to give up, but also the idea of controlling an opponent with a pin or a hold-down in order to effectively secure and apply a finishing hold such as a submission technique. A good hold-down or pin will sap the strength and take the fight out of the guy on bottom, giving the grappler in control a better chance (for the purposes of the subject of this book) of applying a triangle choke.

Holding or pinning an opponent on the ground with the intention of making him surrender is the embodiment of groundfighting or ground grappling. So let's follow Shawn Watson's advice and park him there until he quits

and examine some of the primary holds or pins used to secure a triangle choke.

THE PRIMARY HOLD-DOWNS OR PINS USED TO SECURE TRIANGLE CHOKES

While anything is possible, there are primarily five holding positions that are most often used to control an opponent long enough to secure and apply some type of triangle choke. They are: (1) leg press, (2) mount, (3) side control, (4) scarf hold, and (5) north-south control.

LEG PRESS POSITION

This is one of the strongest grappling positions used in any fighting sport and gives the top fighter or grappler a great amount of control over his opponent. From the leg press, the grappler on top can apply an armlock (often juji gatame—the cross-body armlock), triangle choke, or leglock. Or he may even switch to another controlling pin.

MOUNT OR SCHOOLYARD SIT

The pinning variation of this is called *tate shiho gatame* (vertical four-corner hold) in judo and Japanese jujitsu. The more aggressive fighting version of this controlling position has come to be known as the "mount." It's also been called the "schoolboy sit" or "schoolyard sit" because this position has often been used in schoolyard fights to dominate an opponent. It's also an effective base from which to apply a triangle choke. Every ground-and-pound MMA fighter knows this position quite well.

SIDE CONTROL

What many call side control is also known as *mune gatame* (chest hold) or yoko shiho gatame (side four-corner hold)

in judo and is one of the strongest controlling positions in any form of grappling or fighting. But don't simply think of controlling an opponent from the side as only a pinning situation as used in judo or wrestling. Side control is an ideal holding position to set up an opponent for a variety of submission techniques, including triangle chokes.

SCARF HOLD (HEAD AND ARM PIN)

This is kesa gatame (scarf hold) in judo and variations of it are used in a variety of grappling, fighting, and wrestling sports. Exponents of this pin know very well how to make life miserable for the guy on the bottom, but this is also a good time hold to use to set an opponent up for a triangle choke. In a general sense, the scarf hold or head and arm pin is a variation of side control, as the grappler doing the hold is actually lying at the side of the bottom grappler. However, because of the unique control of the bottom grappler's head, this hold will be considered as a separate pinning or holding position in which to initiate a triangle choke.

NORTH-SOUTH CONTROL

Called kami shiho gatame (upper four-corner hold) in judo and Japanese jujitsu, this controlling hold is ideal to work a triangle choke on an opponent.

TECHNICAL TIP: A hold or pin gives the attacker (1) time and (2) opportunity. Time creates the opportunity. In other words, the control that a hold or pin provides the attacker is the element that gives him more opportunities to secure a triangle choke or other finishing technique. Think of a hold or pin in the same way you do a ride. It is a controlling position. If the attacker controls the position, he or she has a far greater chance of getting the submission.

#1 Roll Back Triangle from Leg Press

The top grappler controls his opponent with a leg press as shown.

The top grappler moves his left foot and may use it to push the bottom grappler's right arm so that more room is created between the bottom grappler's arms and chest. In any case, the top grappler will start to slide and wedge his left foot inside the bottom grappler's right arm.

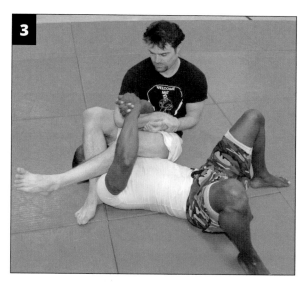

The top grappler slides his left foot and leg deeply through the bottom grappler's arms as shown.

The top grappler moves his right leg so that it is positioned under the bottom grappler's head as shown. As he does this, the top grappler bends his left leg to start to form a triangle.

The top grappler places the top of his left foot behind his right knee as shown. As he does this, the top grappler squeezes with his legs and rolls to his left rear hip area.

This view shows how the top grappler rolls slightly back to his left rear hip. Doing this allows the top grappler to tighten the triangle hold he has created with his feet and legs.

The top grappler may have to continue to roll onto his back left buttocks area to cinch the triangle choke in tightly. As the top grappler rolls to his back left buttocks and hip area, it forces the bottom grappler to roll up, and doing this allows the top grappler to tighten the triangle choke.

The top grappler slides his right foot and lower leg under the bottom grappler's upper back as shown to continue to tighten the triangle choke and get the tap out.

#2 Hip Push Triangle from Leg Press

The top grappler controls his opponent in the leg press as shown.

The top grappler uses his right foot to push on the inside of the bottom grappler's left elbow. Doing this creates an opening between the bottom grappler's arms and torso.

The top grappler slides his right foot and leg through so that it is positioned across the bottom grappler's chest.

The top grappler firmly places his right foot on the mat to hold the bottom man in place as the top grappler starts to move his left foot and leg from across the bottom grappler's chest as shown.

The top grappler places his left foot on the inside (left) hip of the bottom grappler. As he does this, the top grappler uses his left hand to grab the bottom grappler's belt.

The top grappler uses his left hand to pull on his opponent's belt as the top grappler rolls to his left side as shown. As he does this, the top grappler slides his left foot under the upper back of the bottom grappler.

This photo shows how the top grappler slides his left foot and leg under the back of the bottom grappler as the top grappler rolls to his left side. Look at how the top grappler uses his right foot and leg to hook and control the bottom grappler's right arm.

The top grappler forms a triangle by placing the bottom of his right foot behind his left knee.

This photo shows how the top grappler forms the triangle and is positioned on his left side. This is a strong triangle choke, and the attacker can secure the tap out at this point.

If he chooses (and it's highly recommended), the top grappler can secure a juji gatame armlock to get a tap out from both the choke and the armlock in a double trouble situation.

#3 Short Arm Bent Armlock Triangle Choke from the Leg Press

The top grappler controls his opponent with a leg press as shown.

The top grappler moves his right foot and leg across the bottom grappler's torso. Look at how the top grappler uses his hands and arms to trap and control the bottom man's right arm.

The top grappler slides his right foot and leg across the bottom grappler's right lower arm.

The top grappler moves his left leg from across the bottom grappler's face and will slide it under the bottom grappler's head.

As he slides his left upper leg under the bottom grappler's head, the top grappler rolls backward and moves his right foot and leg deeper across the bottom man's right arm as shown.

By rolling backward, the top grappler is better able to slide his left leg under the bottom grappler's head and jam his right foot and leg harder across the bottom grappler's right arm to trap it.

The top grappler forms a triangle by placing the top of his right foot behind his left knee. As he does this, the top grappler squeezes his triangle tighter.

This photo shows the top view of this triangle choke and short arm bent armlock. This is a nasty double trouble situation with both a tight triangle choke and a short arm bent armlock in effect to get the tap out.

#4 Nutcracker Ankle Choke from the Leg Press

The top grappler has controlled his opponent with the leg press and is sliding his right foot and leg under the bottom grappler's right arm as shown.

The top grappler has also moved his leg so that it serves as a pillow to prop the bottom grappler's head and control it. As he does this, the top grappler slides his right foot and leg through as shown.

The top grappler uses his left hand to grab his right ankle. Look at how the top grappler uses his left hand and arm to reach under the bottom grappler's head as the top grappler uses his left hand to grab his ankle. Look at how the top grappler uses his right hand and arm to slide under the bottom grappler's near (right) arm to trap it.

The top grappler uses his left hand to grab his ankle and pull it in tight. The top grappler uses his right hand and arm to wedge on the right side of the bottom grappler's head and neck as the top grappler uses his right hand to grab his left forearm. This forms a tight arm triangle choke and a tight leg choke.

The top grappler has the bottom grappler's head trapped much like a nut that is trapped in a nutcracker with both the arm choke and the leg choke to get the tap out.

#5 Upside Down Triangle Choke from the Leg Press

The top grappler controls his opponent with a leg press.

The top grappler slides his right leg so to move it through the bottom grappler's arms.

The top grappler slides his right foot and leg over the bottom grappler's chest and under his left arm as shown. As he does this, the top grappler forces the bottom grappler to loosen his grip.

The top grappler sits up and forces the bottom grappler to bear the top grappler's weight.

This shows how the top grappler uses his right hand to post on the mat for stability as he sits up.

The top grappler sits up and rolls so that he is posted on the top of his head on the mat for stability. As he does this, the top grappler starts to form a triangle with his feet and legs.

The top grappler places the top of his right foot behind his left knee to form the triangle.

The top grappler rolls to his left as he tightens the triangle to get the tap out.

#6 Can Opener Triangle Choke from Mount

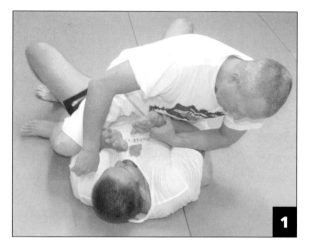

The top grappler controls his opponent with a mount or vertical pin as shown.

The top grappler uses both hands to hook behind the bottom grappler's head to start a can opener neck crank.

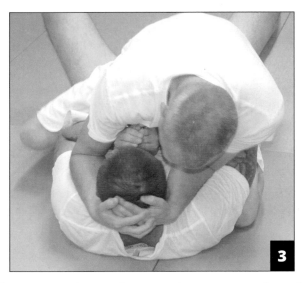

The top grappler can legitimately attempt to force the bottom grappler to tap out with the can opener, but this also allows the top grappler some room to start his triangle.

TECHNICAL TIP: The can opener is a useful submission technique by itself but it can be (and often is) used as an effective way to control an opponent's head when applying a triangle choke.

The top grappler uses both hands to pull up hard on the bottom grappler's head. Doing this allows space for the top grappler to start to move his right foot and leg over the bottom grappler's left shoulder as shown.

The top grappler uses his left hand to grab and pull his right ankle and foot under the bottom grappler's head and shoulders.

The top grappler uses his right hand to grab and pull the bottom grappler's right arm across the bottom man's upper body.

The top grappler continues to use his left hand to pull his right ankle and foot under his opponent as shown as the top man continues to use his right hand to pull the bottom grappler's right arm across his body. Doing this tightens the triangle choke that is forming.

The top grappler forms the triangle with his feet and legs as shown.

The top grappler rolls to his right slightly as he cinches the triangle that he has formed in tighter.

The top grappler continues to roll to his right as he tightens the triangle choke and uses his right hand to continue to pull the bottom grappler's right arm out straight.

The top grappler uses both hands to grab and pull the bottom grappler's extended right arm in a tight armlock as the top grappler uses the triangle to choke his opponent for a double trouble tap out.

#7 Double Arm Trap Triangle Choke from the Mount

The top grappler controls his opponent with a high mount as shown.

The top grappler uses his left hand and arm to grab and push the bottom grappler's right arm across his body.

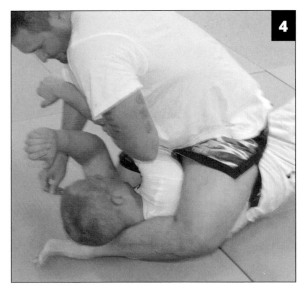

The top grappler rolls to his left slightly so that his left lower leg securely traps the bottom grappler's right shoulder and arm as well as his head.

The top grappler moves his left foot and leg under the bottom grappler's right shoulder.

The top grappler uses his right hand to grab and pull his left ankle or lower leg firmly under his opponent's head.

The top grappler rolls to his left side slightly as he pulls his leg upward in preparation to form the triangle. Look at how both of the bottom grappler's arms are trapped.

The top grappler forms the triangle by using his right hand to pull his left foot up and behind his right knee.

The top grappler has trapped both of his opponent's arms in this tight triangle choke. This results in a tap out.

#8 Knee on Arm Triangle Choke from the Mount

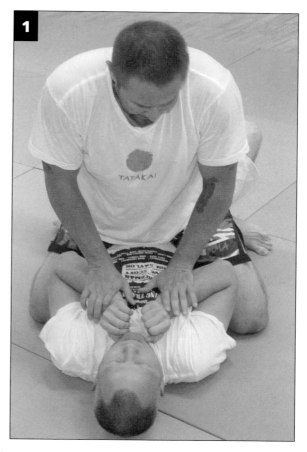

The top grappler controls his opponent with a mount as shown.

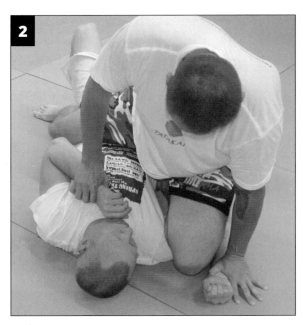

The top grappler moves his left knee up and over the bottom grappler's left upper arm. Doing this traps the bottom grappler's right shoulder and arm.

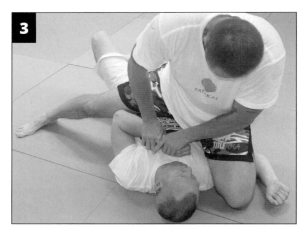

The top grappler uses both hands to grab his opponent's left lower arm as shown. The top grappler extends his right leg for stability.

The top grappler uses both hands to pull the bottom grappler's left arm straight and across his body as shown.

As the top grappler continues to pull on the bottom grappler's left arm, the top grappler moves his right leg up and under his opponent's left shoulder.

The top grappler slides his right foot and lower leg under the bottom grappler's left shoulder and under his head.

The top grappler rolls to his right side in order to help him form the triangle with his feet and legs. Look at how the top grappler uses both hands to pull his opponent's arm out straight.

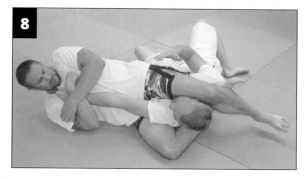

The top grappler forms the triangle by placing the top of his right foot behind his left knee as he uses both hands to pull the bottom grappler's arm straight. The attacker secures the triangle choke as well as the juji gatame armlock to get the tap out with this double trouble situation.

#9 Roll Back Triangle Choke from the Mount

The top grappler controls his opponent with a mount, and the top grappler's right knee traps his opponent's left upper arm.

The top grappler slides his right foot and leg under his opponent's head. The top grappler uses his right hand to grab under the bottom grappler's head to pull it up, allowing the top grappler to slide his right foot and leg under the bottom man's head. The top grappler uses his left hand to grab and pull up on his opponent's right arm.

The top grappler rolls to his back as he uses his left hand to grab and pull his right ankle or lower leg up and under the bottom grappler's head.

The top grappler forms the triangle by placing the top of his right foot behind his left knee as he rolls back.

The top grappler applies the triangle choke as he rolls back and can also apply a straight armlock to get his opponent into double trouble with both the triangle choke and armlock.

#10 Rolling Triangle Choke from the Mount

The top grappler controls his opponent with a mount and uses his right knee to trap the bottom grappler's left upper arm.

The top grappler uses his left hand to grab and pull his opponent's right arm and uses his right hand to hook under the bottom grappler's head. As he does this, the top grappler extends his right leg and posts his right foot on the mat for stability.

The top grappler uses his right hand to pull up on his opponent's head and slides his right foot and leg over the bottom grappler's left shoulder and under his head.

This photo shows how the top grappler uses his right hand to pull up on his opponent's head and slide his right leg under the bottom grappler's head.

The top grappler uses his left hand to grab and pull his right ankle deep under the bottom grappler's head.

The top grappler leans forward to start to form the triangle.

The top grappler rolls over his right shoulder and to his right as he forms the triangle by placing the top of his right foot behind his left knee.

The top grappler continues to roll to his right as he tightens the triangle hold with his feet and legs. Look at how the attacker continues to use his right hand to hold and trap his opponent's right arm.

As the attacker rolls, he tightens the triangle so that when he finishes his roll, the defender taps out from both the triangle choke and the armlock.

#11 Ankle Choke from the Mount

The top grappler controls his opponent with a mount. As he does this, the top grappler uses both hands to grab and trap the bottom grappler's left arm

As he uses his right hand and arm to trap and control the bottom grappler's left arm, the top grappler uses his left hand to grab and pull up on the bottom grappler's head. As he does this, the top grappler moves his right foot and leg forward under the bottom grappler's head.

The top grappler places his right lower leg under his opponent's head and starts to use his left hand to grab his right lower leg or ankle.

The top grappler uses his right hand to reach out and post on the mat as he uses his left hand to grab his right foot.

The top grappler uses his left hand to grab his right foot and slide it up and over the bottom grappler's head so that the attacker's right ankle is jammed on the bottom grappler's throat.

The top grappler leans forward. Doing this applies a lot of pressure to the choke and gets the tap out.

#12 Side Sit-Up Triangle Choke

The attacker (top grappler) controls his opponent from the side as shown. The attacker uses his right arm to hook under the bottom grappler's head and uses his right hand to hook over the bottom grappler's right shoulder. The top grappler uses his right arm to force the bottom grappler's head up.

The attacker posts up on his right foot as he forces the bottom grappler to roll to his right side as shown.

The attacker squats behind his opponent as the top grappler continues to prop the bottom grappler up.

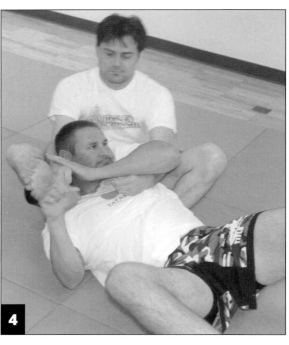

The attacker rolls back so that he is sitting on his buttocks.

The attacker moves his right foot and leg over his opponent's right shoulder. The attacker uses his left hand to grab and pull his right foot and lower leg across the bottom grappler's chest.

The attacker forms a triangle as shown.

The attacker uses his feet and legs to tighten the triangle. This often forces the bottom grappler to tap out from the choke.

The attacker can also use both of his hands and arms to grab the bottom grappler's left arm and apply an armlock as well as a triangle choke.

#13 Side Control Step Over Triangle Choke

This is one of the most common applications of the triangle choke when starting from a side control position.

The top grappler controls his opponent from a side hold or side control position.

The attacker moves his body forward and moves his left foot and leg over the head of the bottom grappler as shown.

The top grappler slides his left foot under the bottom grappler's head and starts to form a triangle.

The top grappler starts to slide his left leg under the bottom grappler's head.

The top grappler forms a triangle with his feet and legs and secures the triangle choke.

#14 Side Control Knee Over Chest to Triangle Choke

The top grappler controls his opponent from the side.

The top grappler starts to move his right knee over and across the bottom grappler's torso.

The top grappler continues to slide his right knee across his opponent's torso. Look at how the top grappler uses his right hand and arm to hook and trap the bottom grappler's left arm.

The top grappler starts to move his right leg over his opponent's torso.

The top grappler moves his right leg over his opponent.

The top grappler moves his right leg so that it is now under the bottom grappler's left armpit area. Look at how the top grappler uses his right hand and arm to trap and pull upward on the bottom grappler's left arm.

The top grappler slides his right foot and leg under the bottom grappler's left shoulder area.

The top grappler starts to form a triangle with his legs as he rolls to his right side as shown.

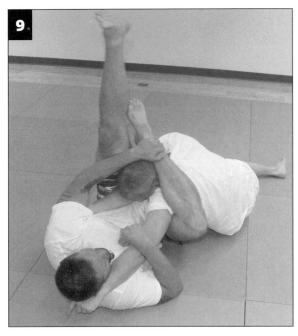

As the attacker rolls to his right, he uses his left hand to grab his right ankle or lower leg to help form the triangle.

As he continues to roll, the attacker securely forms the triangle.

The attacker squeezes with his legs to tighten the triangle as he applies an armlock on his opponent's extended left arm.

#15 Triangle Choke from Kesa Gatame (Scarf Hold or Head and Arm Pin)

The top grappler holds his opponent with kesa gatame as shown.

The top grappler uses his left hand to push down on his opponent's right arm.

The attacker pushes the bottom grappler's right arm down and starts to move his left foot and leg over his opponent's right arm.

The attacker can apply a straight armlock from this position as shown. This also traps the bottom grappler so that the top grappler can continue on to the triangle choke.

The top grappler turns his body to his right as he uses his left hand to hook and pull the bottom grappler's head up and off of the mat as shown.

This photo shows how the attacker uses his right hand and arm to hook under the bottom grappler's left shoulder for additional control.

The top grappler swings his left foot and leg over his opponent's head.

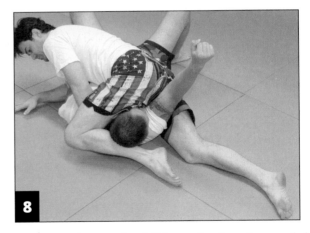

The top grappler uses his left leg to hook and control the bottom grappler's head so that the bottom grappler's head is trapped along with his right arm.

The top grappler forms the triangle by placing the top of his left foot behind his right knee and applies pressure to the triangle choke.

#16 Head-Only Triangle Choke and Headlock from Kesa Gatame

The top grappler controls his opponent with a modified kesa gatame. The top grappler's right hand and arm hook the bottom grappler's left shoulder as shown.

The top grappler starts to swing his left foot and leg up and off of the mat.

The top grappler swings his left foot and leg over his opponent's head as shown.

The top grappler turns to his right and lies on top of his opponent as he uses his left foot and leg to wedge under the bottom grappler's head.

The top grappler forms the triangle by placing the top of his left foot behind his right knee. Look at how the top grappler traps only the head of the bottom grappler and not both his head and arm.

The top grappler tightens the triangle and moves forward so that the bottom grappler's head is cranked up, creating both a choke and a neck crank.

#17 Arm Drag North-South Hold to the Triangle Choke

The top grappler holds his opponent with a north-south hold.

The top grappler uses his right hand to push downward on the bottom grappler's right upper arm. As he does this, the top grappler moves his left knee and lower leg to his left. The top grappler also moves his right foot straight back as shown.

The top grappler moves his left foot and lower leg under the head of the bottom grappler.

The top grappler is sitting on his opponent's upper torso as shown.

The top grappler starts to form the triangle with his feet and legs.

The top grappler forms the triangle by placing the top of his left foot behind his right knee.

The attacker points his right foot upward to cinch the triangle choke in tighter to secure the tap out.

#18 North-South Knee on Arm to Triangle Choke

The attacker holds his opponent with a north-south hold or kami shiho gatame (upper four-corner hold).

The top grappler uses his hands and arms to trap the bottom grappler's left arm and turn the bottom grappler onto his right side as shown.

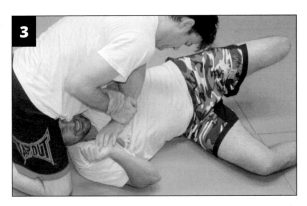

The top grappler can form a keylock or bent armlock. The top grappler can often get the tap out from this bent armlock but this is also a strong controlling position for the top grappler.

The top grappler slides his right knee over onto the bottom grappler's right upper arm.

TECHNICAL TIP: A keylock, top wrist lock, or bent armlock often creates a distraction for the bottom grappler and allows the attacker a strong position of control that can quickly turn into a submission technique if the triangle choke is not successful.

The top grappler uses his right knee and leg to trap the bottom grappler's right upper arm.

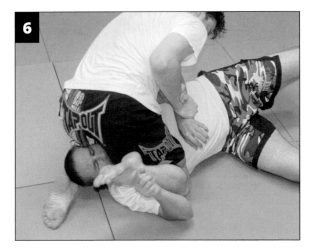

The top grappler moves his left foot and leg under the bottom grappler's head.

The top grappler sits on his opponent's head to control him.

The top grappler starts to move his legs so that they can quickly form a triangle from this position.

The top grappler starts to form the triangle with his feet and legs as shown.

The top grappler secures the triangle choke and can get the tap out at this point.

The attacker can continue on and use his left elbow to wedge on the bottom grappler's right upper leg or thigh. As he does this, the top grappler uses his right hand to grab his opponent's right foot.

The top grappler uses his left hand to grab his opponent's left foot to create a toehold variation to get the tap out with both the triangle choke and the toehold.

The attacker can also turn his right elbow downward and slide it under the bottom grappler's right lower leg so that the lower leg is positioned over the top grappler's right upper arm and shoulder. This creates a strong leg crank to get the tap out along with the triangle choke.

TECHNICAL TIP: The north-south hold or pin is an effective position of control that allows the attacker enough control, position, and space in order to secure a lower body submission technique such as a knee lock, ankle lock, toehold, or heel hook. The attacker's hands and arms are in close proximity to the bottom grappler's feet and legs.

#19 Keylock (or Bent Armlock) from North-South Pin to Triangle Choke

The attacker controls his opponent from this north-south position and can apply a keylock or bent armlock. The attacker (top grappler) squats as shown. Often, the bottom grappler will grab his hands together to prevent the top grappler from applying the bent armlock.

The top grappler jams his left foot and leg over his opponent's head and through the arms of the bottom grappler as shown.

TECHNICAL TIP: The attacker may have to use his left foot to step on the bottom grappler's left upper arm to encourage the bottom grappler to allow the top grappler to step through with his left foot.

This photo shows how the top grappler sits on his opponent's head as he moves forward so that there is no space between his body and the bottom grappler.

The top grappler uses his left hand to grab his opponent's left sleeve as he rolls to his right side. As he does this, the attacker drives his left foot and leg through the arms of the bottom grappler.

The attacker rolls to his right side as he continues to drive his left foot and leg through the bottom grappler's arms. Look at how the bottom grappler's head is lying on the attacker's extended left leg.

The attacker forms the triangle.

The attacker applies pressure to the triangle and secures the choke to get the tap out.

#20 Attacker Sits on Bottom Grappler's Head to Triangle Choke

TECHNICAL TIP: Sometimes, in a scramble, a grappler or fighter will end up sitting on his opponent's chest or upper body. When this takes place, the attacker can take advantage of the situation and turn a neutral scramble into a controlling position to apply the triangle choke.

The top grappler is in a north-south position and is sitting on his opponent's chest.

The top grappler can use his hands and arms to try to apply a lower body submission, and all the while control the bottom grappler with a triangle.

The top grappler forms a triangle from this position by placing the top of his left foot behind his left knee. The

top grappler can lean forward with his opponent's head trapped in the triangle and create a nasty neck crank from this position.

The top grappler can use his hands and arms to grab his opponent and apply a triangle choke from this position. The top grappler can drive his hips forward (in something like a rocking motion), which lifts his legs upward and creates both a nasty choke and an even nastier neck crank on the bottom grappler.

#21 Throw Controlling Position to Triangle Choke

This is a transition from a throw to a controlling north-south position to an immediate triangle choke.

The attacker has just thrown his opponent to the mat and controls him as shown. Look at how the top grappler uses his right hand to hook around his opponent's neck.

The attacker pulls the bottom grappler up off of the mat just enough to give the top grappler room to swing his left foot and leg over the left shoulder of the bottom grappler.

The top grappler swings his left foot and leg over the left shoulder of the bottom grappler as the top grappler rolls to his left side as shown.

The top grappler swings his right foot and leg over and forms the triangle by placing the top of his left foot behind his right knee.

The attacker applies pressure with his legs and secures the triangle choke.

#22 Leg Choke and Neck Crank from Leg Press Position

Credit goes to Sean Daugherty for this leg choke and neck crank when the attacker has an opponent in the leg press position.

The top grappler controls his opponent with a leg press.

The top grappler moves his left foot and leg onto the right biceps of the bottom grappler and pushes the bottom grappler's right upper arm to create space between the bottom man's arms and chest. Doing this creates an opening for the top grappler to slide his leg through.

The top grappler slides his left foot and leg between the defender's arms and chest as shown.

The top grappler moves his left foot and leg over the bottom grappler's chest so that the top grappler's left foot and lower leg will be hooked over the bottom grappler's near (left) shoulder.

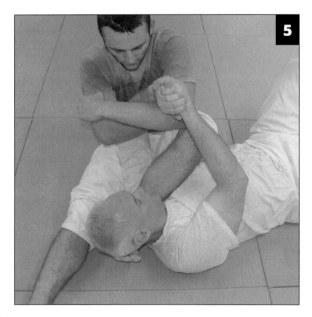

The top grappler uses his left foot and leg to hook over the bottom grappler's left shoulder so that the top grappler's left shin is jammed tightly against the left side of the bottom grappler's neck.

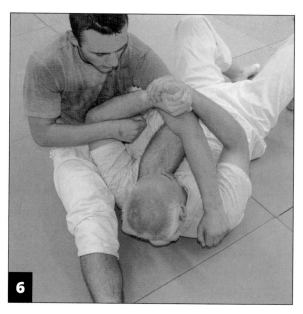

The top grappler uses his left hand and arm to reach forward to start to grab the bottom grappler's head. Look at how the top grappler has his left shin and lower leg jammed tightly against the left side of the bottom grappler's neck and how the top grappler uses his left foot to hook and control the bottom grappler's head.

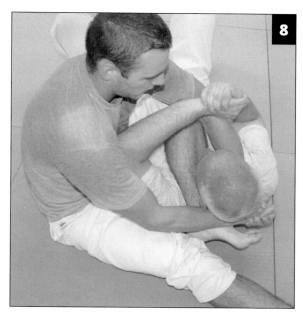

The top grappler uses his left shin and lower leg to jam and push against the left side of the bottom grappler's neck. As he does this, the top grappler uses his hands and arms to trap and pull the bottom grappler's head in tightly. Doing this creates a nasty leg choke as well as a nasty neck crank.

The top grappler grabs his hands together and forms a square (Gable) grip. Look at how the top grappler's left forearm is wedged tightly against the right side of the bottom grappler's neck and how the top grappler's square grip is used to lift up on the bottom man's head.

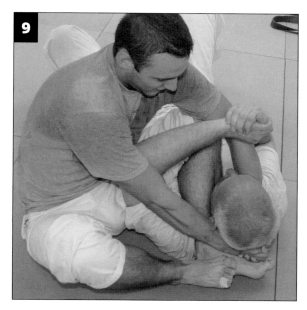

To add more pressure to the choke and neck crank, the top grappler places the bottom of his right foot on the heel of his left foot and pushes. Doing this adds more power to the choke and gets an immediate tap out.

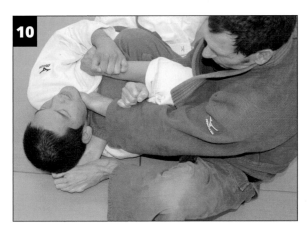

In a situation where the grapplers are wearing jackets, the top grappler can also use his left hand to grab the left side of the bottom grappler's jacket as shown to create an effective leg and lapel choke.

TECHNICAL TIP: It can't be emphasized enough: time creates opportunity. A "time hold" is a secure and strong starting position that allows a grappler or fighter the opportunity to secure a triangle choke. It is a position where the defender is usually on his or her back or side with the attacker in control. Take what has been presented in this chapter and experiment with a variety of holds and pins to see how many different ways a triangle choke can be applied from these strong controlling positions.

So far, a variety of triangle chokes have been presented from four primary positional situations: (1) starting from the bottom guard, (2) starting from in front of an opponent, (3) starting from a rodeo ride, and (4) starting from one of several holding or pinning positions. In the next chapter, defenses and escapes will be presented. Knowing how to get an opponent into a triangle choke will end the fight, but if you are on the receiving end of a triangle choke, knowing how to defend and escape from a triangle choke will keep you in the fight. Let's get started.

Part 6: Prevention, Defenses, and Escapes

TRIANGLE CHOKE PREVENTION, DEFENSES, AND ESCAPES

The first few pages of this chapter will examine some basic concepts of preventing, defending, and escaping from triangle chokes. After that, more specific methods of prevention, defense, and escaping will be presented.

There are some common factors used when preventing, evading, defending, escaping, or countering a triangle choke attack. Fundamentally, the first phase is to prevent an attack from happening or negate the attack when initially recognized or before the attack takes place. The second phase is actively defending against an opponent who is attempting to apply a triangle choke. For whatever reason, the defender has been unable to prevent the attack or possibly didn't realize the attack was taking place. In this case, a solid defense is necessary to stay in the fight. The third phase takes place if the defender has been caught in the triangle and must escape from it. Needless to say, this is a tough situation, but keeping cool and knowing what to do may be the tools necessary to escape from a bad situation.

PREVENTION

The best way to get out of a triangle is not to get into one and to stop it before it starts, but that is sometimes easier said than done. As presented in the earlier chapters of this book, a fighter or grappler who is skilled at triangle chokes will control the position in order to set up the application of the choke. Recognizing that an opponent is starting to develop a triangle and knowing what to look for are skills only developed through constant and structured training and through a lot of experience actually grappling or fighting on the mat. Knowing how to negate or prevent an opponent from establishing a controlling position is a skill that every grappler should have, and this takes constant, regular, and structured training. Being able to realize that a bad situation is developing is an important asset that every fighter or grappler must possess. A good way to prevent an opponent from attacking with a triangle choke is to constantly put him on the defensive. A good offense is indeed the best defense, but when fighting a fit, motivated, and skilled opponent, the ability to see when he is attempting to mount his offense is a skill that comes from hard, smart training and experience.

There are several specific preventive measures a defender must take to ensure that he isn't caught in a triangle choke. They are: (1) The defender recognizes that the attacker is setting him up, and he or she takes evasive action to control the position to prevent the situation from worsening. (2) The defender must prevent his opponent from forming a triangle, or if the opponent has already started to form the triangle with his legs, the defender must halt its progress and keep the opponent from hooking his leg over the defender's head. Posture up, keep the shoulders in tightly and compactly, and do not let the opponent get his foot or leg over your upper arm or shoulder. Above all, control your head and don't let your opponent hook his leg over your head. (3) Preemptive attack: the defender immediately attacks as his opponent attempts to apply the triangle, beating him to the punch (maybe not the punch, but certainly beating him to the choke).

DEFENSE

If an opponent is able to start his triangle attack, it is vital to act quickly and put up a good defense. It's a simple fact that it takes two to tango and the ability to defend oneself is a necessary skill.

The position (and who controls it) is a fundamental aspect of grappling and fighting. If the attacker controls the position, the defender should do everything possible to get involved in a scramble. A scramble is a grappling situation where neither athlete has an advantage. So, if you are unable to control the position then at least get into a scramble situation so the opponent has less control and does not control the position.

The defender should immediately get his arms inside the attacker's legs so the attacker can't form a triangle with his feet and legs. This is a proactive defense as it affords fewer gaps and holes for the attacker to wedge his foot or leg in to start the triangle. It's proactive in the sense that the defender can quickly take aggressive action from this position to counter the opponent.

A major rule is that at no time should a grappler or fighter lie flat on his front. Some people think lying flat on the front in this way is "safe." But in this position the defender has no real chance of doing anything other than hoping that the referee will call a halt to the action.

ESCAPES

If a grappler or fighter gets caught in a triangle, he must immediately realize his predicament, keep calm, and do everything allowed within the rules of the sport to escape. Regular and structured drill training on both defense and escape methods are necessary for every grappler or fighter, and working on defenses for the triangle choke should be drilled on enough that a grappler can instinctively react effectively when caught in a compromising situation.

Also, realize that an escape doesn't always lead to a situation where a counter-attack can be made. Sometimes, just getting out of trouble and surviving the immediate threat is enough to keep a grappler in the match or fight.

TECHNICAL TIP: When defending or escaping from a triangle choke, think logically and keep your cool. Keep things simple and get out of trouble. Often your defensive move will put you in position to better make your escape. Don't try some flashy or complicated technique simply because some famous fighter has done it. It's your neck on the line right now, not his.

PREVENT THE TRIANGLE: KEY POINTS

THE DEFENDER MUST CONTROL HIS OPPONENT'S HIPS

The legs are connected to the hips, so it makes sense for the defender to control his opponent's hips to prevent the attacker from forming a triangle with his legs.

HANDS ON HIPS

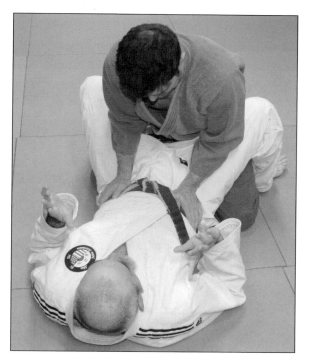

The top grappler uses both hands to press down firmly on the bottom grappler's hips, pinning them to the mat. Doing this controls the mobility of the bottom grappler's hips and legs and prevents the triangle from starting in most cases.

POSTURE UP

The bottom grappler (the attacker in this photo) wants to use one of his legs to hook over the top grappler's shoulder and head in order to pull him down low and start to form the triangle. This initial hooking leg is the anchor leg in the formation of the triangle, and the top grappler makes sure to "posture up" to prevent the bottom grappler from hooking with either leg to start his triangle.

ATTACKER WANTS TO CONTROL OPPONENT'S HEAD

This photo shows how the attacker (on bottom) has used his right leg to hook and control his opponent's head to start his triangle choke. The bottom grappler wants to use his right leg to hook and pull the top grappler's head down low enough so that the bottom grappler can start to form the triangle with his feet and legs. It is essential for the top grappler (the defender in this photo) to prevent his opponent from pulling his head down and breaking his posture forward. This is why it is important to "posture up" and maintain a strong upright posture when in the top guard position.

DEFENDER PREVENTS OPPONENT FROM CONTROLLING HIS ARM, SHOULDER, OR HEAD

In keeping with the two previous photos, the defender must not allow the attacker to control his head. As previously mentioned, the attacker wants to hook and control the defender's upper arm, shoulder, or head so that he can go on to form the triangle. By posturing up and keeping the attacker from hooking his leg over the upper arm, shoulder, or head, the defender (top grappler in this photo) can better prevent the triangle from being formed. Sometimes, the simplest thing to do can be the best. This photo shows the top grappler using his hands and arms to block the bottom grappler's leg from hooking the top grappler's arm, shoulder, or head.

> **TECHNICAL TIP: Simple things done right are called "fundamentals," and fundamentals done right win fights.**

Some specific ways of doing this are presented in the following photos.

ARMS INSIDE AND BELOW OPPONENT'S LEGS

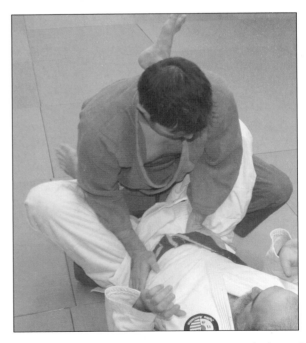

To form a triangle choke, the bottom grappler's goal is to get one leg over the top grappler's arm, shoulder, and neck. To prevent this, the top grappler must make sure to keep his opponent's legs outside and below his arms.

TECHNICAL TIP: By keeping the attacker's legs below his arms and shoulders, the defender can better prevent his opponent from forming a triangle around his shoulder, head, and neck.

BELT GRIP AND HIP CONTROL

The top grappler uses his hands to grab the bottom grappler's belt and uses his forearms and elbows to block the bottom grappler's legs near his hips. This inside thigh control near the bottom grappler's legs can often isolate them and prevent the bottom grappler from starting to form a triangle with his legs.

TOP GRAPPLER USES HIS ELBOW TO BLOCK BOTTOM GRAPPLER'S ANCHOR LEG

To prevent the bottom grappler from forming a triangle, the top grappler aggressively uses his right forearm and elbow to jam and block inside the bottom grappler's left leg. This prevents the bottom grappler from using his left leg to hook over the top grappler's head as an anchor leg to start to form his triangle. Look at how the top grappler grabs his opponent's belt at the crotch area with his palms up. In the same way a person uses the palm up grip to curl a barbell, this palm-up grip on the bottom grappler's belt gives the top grappler additional leverage and strength to control and manipulate his opponent.

PALM-DOWN BELT GRAB IS ALSO ACCEPTABLE

The important thing is for the top grappler to control the bottom grappler in the middle of his body (at the crotch or abdomen area) and for the top grappler to use his forearms and elbows to prevent the bottom man from using his legs. If the top grappler happens to grab in a palm down position, that's okay too.

DEFENDER MUST BE READY TO BLOCK EITHER LEG

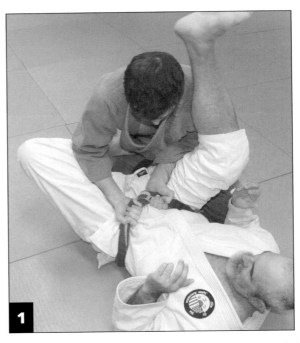

The top grappler uses his elbows to block and his shoulders to roll off and block the bottom grappler's legs. If the bottom grappler initially uses his right leg to attack with the triangle, he may quickly use his other leg if his right leg gets blocked.

As the bottom grappler uses his left leg, the top grappler must quickly block it.

STACK AND STOP

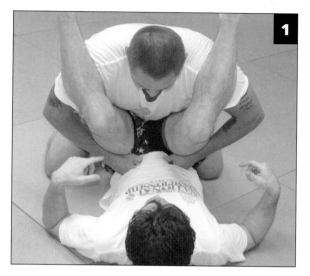

Sometimes, the top grappler will have to use his hands and arms to grab and pull the bottom grappler's upper legs and hips up so the bottom grappler is stacked on his shoulders and head.

As he stacks the bottom grappler, the top grappler can quickly get past his legs to gain control.

DEFENSE AGAINST THE TRIANGLE: KEY POINTS

If the defender has been unable to prevent the attacker from using his anchor leg to hook over the head or shoulder, the defender will have to get rid of the attacker's anchor leg. Presented here are some basic techniques the defender can use to get rid of the attacker's anchor leg.

DEFENDER STOPS ATTACKER FROM USING A LEG TO CONTROL HIS HEAD

The attacker wants to establish an anchor leg to hook and control the defender's head, arm, or shoulder. This is an important step in developing the triangle. As mentioned previously, it is essential that the defender prevent his opponent from using the anchor leg to hook and control his head.

LEG SHUCK

Sometimes, the bottom grappler is able to use his foot and leg to hook over the head of the top grappler. In this situation, the top grappler must use both hands (or either hand) and his arm to grab the bottom grappler's leg.

The top grappler grabs and pulls the bottom grappler's leg over his head and defends himself from the triangle.

SWIM THROUGH AND ROLL

The bottom grappler uses her hands and arms to "swim" or slide through the foot and leg of the top grappler as he attempts to form the triangle from the front position.

In many situations, the bottom grappler can drive forward (swim through) and roll to one side to continue to prevent the top grappler from hooking his feet and legs together to form the triangle.

This photo shows how the bottom grappler must continue to roll through aggressively to defend against the formation of the triangle choke.

HEEL PEEL AND BREAK OPEN DEFENSE

If the top grappler (the attacker) is able to use his left leg (in this photo) to hook under the bottom grappler's arm to start the triangle, the bottom grappler can use a "heel peel" to negate the development of the triangle.

The top grappler has managed to use his left foot and leg to hook under the right arm of the bottom grappler to start the triangle choke. The bottom grappler uses his right hand to grab the left heel of the top grappler and pull it away so that the attacker's left foot cannot form the triangle.

PRE-EMPTIVE ATTACK

As mentioned previously, a good offense is a good defense and this proves it. There will be more on this later in this chapter, but if the defender can immediately counter-attack as the opponent initially attempts the triangle choke, the defender can turn a bad situation into a good one.

The top grappler starts his triangle choke.

The bottom grappler aggressively drives into her opponent and uses a double-leg grab (or a single-leg grab) to counter the top grappler's triangle choke.

The bottom grappler continues to drive forward and "break open" the triangle that the top grappler attempted to form with his feet and legs. The defender can forcefully posture up as shown in this photo to throw the top grappler over the bottom man's back.

TECHNICAL TIP: The Japanese have an old concept called "*kobo ichi*" that translates into the idea of an "aggressive defense" or turning a defensive move into an aggressive counter move. Kobo ichi is a fluid concept of defense-offense with the athlete defending as necessary, and always looking for an opening to attack.

Realistically, in some cases, you will be happy to defend or escape and survive to fight another day, but whenever possible, make every effort to turn the situation around and go on offense. In every situation presented in this chapter, keep kobo ichi in mind and look at how the skills presented in this chapter can be turned into an offensive move. (For a more comprehensive explanation and discussion of kobo ichi, refer to my book refer to my book *The Judo Advantage* published by YMAA Publications.)

ESCAPES FROM TRIANGLE: KEY POINTS

Get out of trouble first, then think about countering the opponent

Presented here are some basic ways for the defender to escape from a triangle choke.

DEFENDER STALLS ACTION AND CREATES SPACE

This photo shows how the defender (left) uses his right foot and leg to push against his opponent to create enough space to impede the action of the triangle choke.

DEFENDER TURNS OR TWISTS TO LESSEN THE EFFECT OF THE CHOKE AND ESCAPE

In some situations, the defender will have to twist or spin his body over to stop the bottom grappler's triangle from developing any further.

DEFENDER STANDS UP

Sometimes, the best way to escape from a triangle choke is for the top grappler to stand up and lift the bottom up off of the mat. In some sports (like judo or some forms of sport jujitsu), lifting the bottom grappler up off of the mat will stop the action. In other sports (such as MMA or submission grappling), the action does not stop so the top grappler must do something like drive or spike the bottom grappler back down to the mat.

PREVENTION, DEFENSE, AND ESCAPE FROM TRIANGLE CHOKES

Up to this point, we have examined some of the basic concepts of prevention, defense, and escape from triangle chokes. Now it's time to put these concepts together and examine some specific skills of prevention, defense, and escape for getting out of trouble when an opponent tries to apply a triangle choke.

#1 Isolate Hips, Split Bottom Grappler's Legs Wide to Prevent Triangle Choke and Leg Pass

The top grappler uses his hands to push down on the bottom grappler's hips to pin them to the mat and prevent him from starting a triangle choke.

The top grappler pops up so he is posting on his left foot as shown. Doing this traps the bottom grappler's right leg.

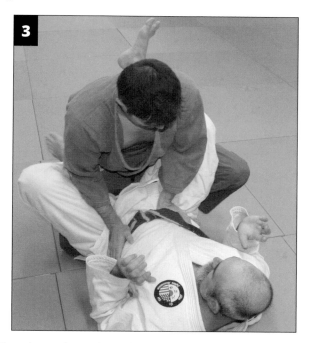

This photo shows how the top grappler traps the bottom grappler's right leg.

4

The top grappler quickly drives his right knee and shin over and onto the bottom grappler's left upper thigh.

5

The top grappler uses his left hand and arm to hook under the bottom grappler's right leg. The top grappler uses his left hand and arm to trap the bottom grappler's right knee as shown. Look at how the top grappler uses his right knee to drive down and split the bottom grappler's legs wide apart.

6

The top grappler quickly uses his hands and arms to allow his body to slide on the outside and past the bottom grappler's right leg as shown.

7

The top grappler is now on the outside and at the right side of the bottom grappler.

The top grappler quickly moves to his left and past the bottom grappler's right leg to take control.

#2 Knee on Crotch to Prevent Triangle and Leg Pass to Prevent Triangle Choke

This move will not make friends for anyone who uses it. Basically, the top grappler jams his (in this photo) right knee or shin in the middle of his opponent's crotch, placing a lot of pressure on the bottom grappler's testicles. This tends to make the bottom grappler focus on this and draw his attention away from the top grappler's attempt to pass the bottom grappler's guard.

The top grappler uses his left hand to grab on the inside of the bottom grappler's right knee. As he does this, the top grappler uses his right knee and shin to jam down hard on the bottom grappler's crotch or upper thigh.

The top grappler pops up so that he is squatting as shown. As he does this, the top grappler starts to use his left hand and arm to hook under the bottom grappler's right leg.

The top grappler uses his left hand and arm to hook and control the bottom man's right lower leg, and as he does this, the top grappler starts to swing the bottom grappler's right leg past his body as shown.

The top grappler uses his left hand and arm to swing the bottom grappler's right leg to the top grappler's right. Doing this allows the top grappler to quickly pass by the bottom grappler's right side.

The top grappler moves to his left and controls the top grappler from the side as shown.

#3 Isolate Upper Leg, Head Shuck, and Leg Pass to Prevent Triangle Choke

The top grappler uses both hands to grab on the inside of the bottom grappler's knees and drive them down hard to the mat. Doing this splits the bottom grappler's legs wide open. As he does so, the top grappler drives his left knee and shin onto the crotch of the bottom grappler.

The top grappler uses his left knee and shin to drive down hard and slide past the bottom grappler's right upper leg and thigh. As he does this, the top grappler uses his right hand, elbow, and arm to block the bottom grappler's left leg and prevent it from starting to form a triangle.

The top grappler uses both of his hands and arms to grab and pull the bottom grappler's left foot and leg over the top of his head. If necessary, the top grappler may have to use his hands and arms to grab and push the bottom grappler's left foot and leg from behind the top grappler's head to prevent the bottom grappler from forming a triangle.

The top grappler uses both of his hands and arms to pull and control the bottom grappler's left leg. The top grappler pushes the bottom grappler's left leg to the mat across the bottom grappler's body as shown.

The top grappler moves to his right to gain side control.

#4 Elbow Block to Knee on Thigh to Prevent Triangle Choke

The top grappler uses his left elbow and upper arm to block the bottom grappler from starting to form a triangle as shown. Look at how the top grappler has already used both of his hands to grab and control the bottom grappler's belt. Doing this controls the bottom grappler's hips and limits the movement of the bottom grappler's hips and legs.

The top grappler quickly slides his right knee and shin over the left knee and thigh of the bottom grappler.

The top grappler moves to his right and across the bottom grappler's trapped left upper leg.

The top grappler continues to move to his right to pass the left leg and hip of the bottom grappler.

The top grappler moves to his right to gain side control.

The top grappler gains side control and pins his opponent.

#5 Block Attacker's Leg and Pass Guard to Prevent Triangle Choke

In many situations, the best thing to do to prevent an opponent from starting a triangle choke is to simply use the hands and arms to block the leg and prevent it from starting the triangle.

The bottom grappler starts to form the triangle with his right leg as shown. The top grappler quickly uses his left hand and arm to block the bottom grappler's right leg as shown.

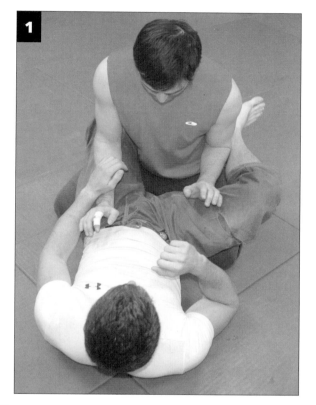

The top grappler is in the guard of the bottom grappler.

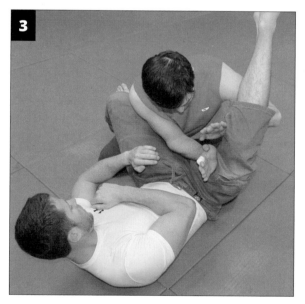

The top grappler can use both hands and arms to drive on the inside of the bottom grappler's right leg so that the leg is pushed down and to the mat.

The top grappler uses his hands and arms to continue to drive the bottom grappler's right leg down to the mat.

The top grappler uses both of his hands and arms to pin the bottom grappler's right leg to the mat as shown.

The top grappler slides his left knee and lower leg over the top of the bottom grappler's trapped right leg as shown. The top grappler sits on the bottom grappler's right upper leg and pins him to the mat.

The top grappler starts to move to his left and use his left lower leg to trap the bottom grappler's right leg and pin it to the mat.

The top grappler uses his right foot to trap the bottom grappler's lower right leg. Doing this completely traps and pins the bottom grappler's right leg to the mat.

The top grappler continues to move to his left and gets past the bottom grappler's right leg.

The top grappler gains side control.

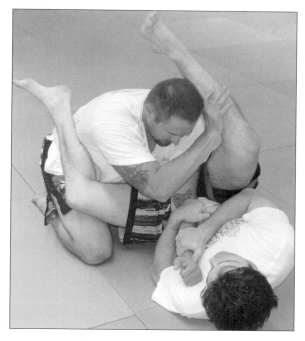

TECHNICAL TIP: Much the same way a boxer keeps his head low and shoulders shrugged, it's a good idea for a grappler to keep his chin tucked with his head low and shoulders shrugged to better prevent an opponent from hooking his leg over the defender's shoulder and head. By keeping your chin tucked, it's much easier to block or parry an opponent's leg, preventing him from forming a triangle.

#6 Stack and Pass Defense Against Triangle Choke

The top grappler uses both hands and arms to grab, scoop, and pull both of the upper legs of the bottom grappler. Doing this pulls and stacks the bottom grappler up and onto his upper back and neck.

The top grappler starts to move to his left as he continues to stack the bottom grappler high on his upper back and shoulders.

As he moves to his left, the top grappler swings both of the legs of the bottom grappler to the top grappler's right. Doing this allows the top grappler to pass to his left and past the right side of the bottom grappler.

The top grappler moves to the side and gains control.

#7 Straight Knee Lock Defense Against Triangle Choke

The top grappler uses his left arm to trap the bottom grappler's right leg (just at the kneecap) as the bottom grappler attempts to use his right leg to form the triangle.

The top grappler moves to his left as he grabs his hands together in a square grip and secures a straight leg lock.

#8 Hug Leg and Spin-Over Escape from Triangle Choke

hands to grab and hug the right upper leg of the bottom grappler.

As he hugs the bottom grappler's right upper leg, the top grappler moves to his left.

The bottom grappler secures a triangle choke. The top grappler quickly bends forward and uses both

The top grappler continues to move to his left and "rolls" out of the triangle choke.

The top grappler continues to move to his left and shucks or pulls the bottom grappler's right leg over his head to get past the bottom grappler's right leg.

The top grappler moves to his left to gain side control.

#9 Stack and Pass Escape from Triangle Choke

The top grappler has been caught in a triangle choke by the bottom grappler.

The top grappler quickly stands up and leans forward so that he forces the bottom grappler to be placed on his upper back and head as shown.

This photo shows how the top grappler stands up and "stacks" the bottom grappler. The top grappler may have to use his left hand to post on the mat for stability as he stands.

The top grappler pulls his head free and moves to his left and over the bottom grappler's right hip and leg as shown.

The top grappler can now pass by the right leg and hip of the bottom grappler to take control.

#10 Twist-Over Escape from Triangle Choke

The bottom grappler has a triangle choke formed and controls the top grappler.

The top grappler stands up, and as he does this, he leans forward to attempt to loosen the effect of the triangle choke.

The top grappler sits on his buttocks and quickly slides his right foot forward.

The top grappler twists his body to his left.

The top grappler aggressively continues to twist his body to his left. As he does this, he turns the bottom grappler over as shown.

The top grappler continues to twist and turn his body to his left so that he twists out of the triangle choke.

#11 Leg Push Escape from Triangle Choke

The bottom grappler has a firm triangle choke applied from the bottom as shown.

The top grappler rolls to his left hip and starts to move his right leg up and forward as shown.

The top grappler uses his right foot and leg to jam under the bottom grappler's left armpit area to create space between the grappler's bodies.

The top grappler uses his right foot and leg to drive hard against the left armpit area of the bottom grappler. Doing this can make space between the bodies of the grapplers and loosen the triangle choke.

As the top grappler drives with his right foot against the armpit area of the bottom grappler, the top grappler pulls his body away to loosen the triangle choke.

The top grappler immediately works to get side control of the bottom grappler after the top grappler escapes.

#12 Break Open and Crawl Through

The top grappler secures his left foot and leg over the right shoulder of the bottom grappler to start his triangle.

The bottom grappler immediately drives forward and uses his right arm to drive sideways to "break open" the triangle of the top grappler.

As he drives forward, the bottom grappler postures up so the top grappler falls over his back as shown.

#13 Swim Through and Roll to Counter Pin

The top grappler sinks his left foot and leg in to control the bottom grappler's right arm and shoulder as shown.

The bottom grappler uses her right hand to grab the left heel of the top grappler. As she does this, the bottom grappler uses her left hand to slide on the inside of the top grappler's right leg just above the knee.

The bottom grappler "swims through" with her hands and arms and moves forward as she forcefully rolls to her right as shown.

This photo shows how the bottom grappler forcefully rolls to her right side.

The bottom grappler rolls through so she rolls over as shown. As she does this, the bottom grappler continues to use her hands and arms to wedge apart her opponent's legs as shown.

The defender continues to roll and continues to wedge her opponent's legs apart as she rolls.

The defender continues to roll over and on top of her opponent as shown.

The defender completes her roll and secures a pin as a counter-technique.

#14 Heel Peel and Break Open Defense

1

The top grappler sinks in his left foot and leg over the bottom grappler's right arm as shown.

2

The bottom grappler uses his right hand to grab the left heel of the top grappler and pull (peel) it away so that the top grappler is unable to form a triangle. As he does this, the bottom grappler immediately moves forward forcefully. Doing this forces the top grappler to fall forward as shown.

The bottom grappler "breaks open" by using both of his hands and arms to pull the feet and legs of the top grappler apart. Doing this stops the triangle choke.

#15 Pre-emptive Double Leg Attack Against Triangle Choke

The top grappler attacks the bottom grappler with a front triangle choke.

The bottom grappler immediately counters by driving in forcefully with a double leg (or single leg) breakdown. The bottom grappler must take pre-emptive action and aggressively counter attack the top grappler.

The bottom grappler breaks her opponent to the mat and quickly gets to a side control position.

The defender has countered her opponent and successfully controls her opponent from the side.

"The greatest pleasure in life is doing what people say you can't do."
Walter Bagehot

Part 7: Epilogue

SOME FINAL TOUGHTS

Efficiency is one of the primary characteristics of success. An effective move is an effective move no matter what it is called, who invented it, or in what fighting sport it is used. The triangle choke proves this point.

In the competitive world of fighting sports, the skills that work and work with a high ratio of success stand the test of time. Efficiency in executing skills is dependent on two other factors: (1) a willingness to fight and take the risks that are part of it and (2) the fitness necessary to execute skills at a high level.

As with my other books, I'll kick myself for neglecting to include something after seeing this book in print, so with that in mind, allow me to apologize for not including more. But hopefully the skills that have been presented on these pages will stimulate further thought and innovation on the part of every reader.

It's always been my belief that authors' words speak to us from the pages of books for many years. Our favorite authors continue to speak to us even though they may be deceased. Their written words speak to us as long as we continue to read them. And as we grow and improve in our appreciation for a given subject, we gain new insight as we read and reread what has been written. It is my hope as an author that every reader will gain something worthwhile each time he or she reads what I have written.

Steve Scott
Kansas City, Missouri

GLOSSARY

Presented here are some often-used names, terms, and phrases, many of which appear in this book.

Anchor: An anchor is the hand, foot, or any body part of a grappler used to stabilize any body part of his opponent.

Anchor Foot or Leg: The foot or leg that a grappler uses to initially hook, trap, and control an opponent. (See "Tie-Up Leg or Foot.")

Back Fighter or Back Grappler: A grappler who is positioned below or under his opponent. This describes a grappler who prefers to fight off of his backside as in newaza or the guard position.

Back Fighting (also called the Guard or Fighting from the Butt): This is an old position from the early days of Japanese judo called newaza. Newaza means "reclining or supine techniques" and is a useful position for both top and bottom grapplers.

Beltline: This refers to the midsection and hip area of the body where one wears a belt.

Block (or Check or Tap): A block is the use of a hand, foot, or other body part to stop or control the movement of any body part of an opponent. A block is also called a check or a tap.

Bottom Grappler: The grappler or fighter who is on the bottom in groundfighting or ground grappling.

Breakdown: A breakdown is a skill that takes an opponent from a stable to an unstable position.

Bridge: A bridge takes place when a grappler who is lying on his back arches up off of his head and shoulders and feet at the same time.

Can Opener: A neck crank where the attacker uses one or both hands to pull his opponent's head forward causing pain. In more generic terms, a can opener is also any prying movement where one fighter or grappler causes pain to secure a move.

Choke: A specific action where the trachea is attacked by squeezing or constriction. Any blockage of the throat at the windpipe is considered a choke. The word "choke" is often used in place of the word "strangle" when describing a submission technique aimed at the throat. (See "Strangle.")

Crank: A crank take place any time a grappler takes an opponent's joint or body part out of its normal range of motion or movement.

Dead: A body part that is not useful to the grappler is sometimes called "dead."

Dojime: This phrase literally means "body squeeze or constriction." A dojime is when one grappler entwines his legs around an opponent's body and constricts or squeezes him, forcing him to submit or at least control the opponent's movement.

Drag: A drag is when a grappler pulls an opponent's hand, arm, leg, foot, or any body part to control it.

Escape: When a grappler is able to get out of any hold or technique, he has escaped it.

Finishing Hold: Any hold or technique designed to force an opponent to surrender or submit. This is another name for a submission technique.

Grapevine: When one grappler entwines or wraps his legs around an opponent's legs. The term grapevine more often refers specifically to entwining and controlling an opponent's legs to stretch them out.

Groundfighting: Engaging an opponent or assailant on the ground or mat, including the use of pins, chokes, armlocks, leg or ankle locks, neck or head locks, punching, kicking, or any offensive or defensive technique or finishing hold. Groundfighting is often used as a generic term for any form of grappling or fighting on the ground or mat.

Ground Grappling: This term refers to the variation of groundfighting that excludes striking techniques. Ground grappling is the sport variation of groundfighting or groundwork.

Groundwork: Another generic term for any groundfighting or grappling on the ground.

Guard: A specific position used in grappling and fighting where the bottom grappler fights from a supine position. (See "Newaza.")

Heist: To "steal" or control any part of an opponent's body. An example is a "hip heist" where one grappler controls the hip of his opponent.

Kill: When one grappler nullifies or controls an opponent's body part. An example is when one grappler traps, hooks, or controls his opponent's arm, making it useless to the opponent—that is, "killing" his arm.

Lace or Lacing: We call the action "lacing" when the bottom grappler wraps or entwines his leg or leg around hip opponent's leg or legs from the bottom (ground or mat) up.

Leg Press: A specific position of control in grappling or fighting where the attacker is positioned on his buttocks next to his opponent with the attacker on top and with his legs extended over the bottom fighter's upper body. The top fighter uses his legs to control the bottom fighter.

Lever: The act of prying and manipulating an opponent's arm so it loosens the opponent's grip. This often is used when describing how the attacking grappler straightens his opponent's arm to apply juji gatame (cross-body armlock).

Mount: A specific controlling position used in combat sports where the attacker is positioned sitting on the defender's chest with the defender lying on his back. This position has also been called a "schoolyard sit" or "schoolboy sit" and is a fighting variation of tate shiho gatame (vertical four-corner hold).

Newaza: The Japanese name used to describe what is now commonly called the "guard." Specifically, this word is translated as "supine or reclining techniques." In some Japanese texts, this position is also called "newaza no semekata" which translates to "attacking forms from a supine position."

Pick: When a grappler uses his hand to grab or hook an opponent's ankle, foot, leg, wrist, hand, or arm and quickly pulls it.

Post: When a grappler uses a hand, foot, or any part of his body to place on the mat to stabilize himself.

Ride: A temporary controlling position where one grappler maintains a dominant position over his opponent.

Sankaku Jime: The Japanese name that translates to "triangle choke." Specifically, the word "sankaku" translates to "triangle" or "three corners." In some cases, the word "sangaku" is used because the "k" sound in the word "kaku" hardens to a "g" sound when used as the second word in a name. The word "jime" translates to "to tighten, squeeze, or constrict." (See "Shime Waza.")

Scissors: When a grappler entwines his legs, often hooking his ankles, to control any part of his opponent's body and often to apply pressure to squeeze or constrict a body part to force the opponent to submit.

Scramble: An often neutral situation or position where neither grappler has control and they work to take control of the position and control the opponent.

Shime Waza: The Japanese name for a strangling or choking technique. Specifically, "shime" is tranlated as "tighten, squeeze, or constrict." When used as the second word in a name or phrase such as "sankaku jime," the "sh" sound is hardened to a "j" sound. The word "waza" means "technique" or "skill."

Shoot: When the grapplers are not holding onto each other in a standing position, there is some space between the bodies of the grapplers, and one grappler dives in low to attempt a takedown or transition.

Shuck: The act of pushing, manipulating, or quickly moving an opponent's hand, arm, leg, foot, or any body part.

Side Control: Controlling an opponent when the defender is lying on his back or backside and the attacker is positioned at his side in a control or holding position. This is a useful position used in grappling and fighting sports.

Snap Down: This takes place when one grappler quickly pulls his opponent's head and upper body down to the mat.

Sprawl: A basic move in wrestling and useful in all types of sport combat, the grappler flattens out with his legs wide, often driving his hip and torso down on the grappler who is shooting in for a takedown.

Shrimp: A bending or curling of the grappler's body when he is on his back or side to propel himself on the mat. The grappler's body resembles a shrimp.

Stack: Pulling an opponent up onto his shoulders and neck and placing the weight of his body on them to control him.

Strangle: The generic name for any submission technique aimed at the neck or throat. A strangle also refers to any submission technique attacking the carotid arteries.

Submission Technique: Any skill or technique that forces an opponent to submit. (See "Finishing Hold.")

Sweep: Any time a grappler uses his foot, leg, hand, arm, or any body part to quickly move and control an opponent's feet, legs, hands, arms, or any body part. A foot sweep is a good example.

Swim: When a grappler slides or moves his hand, arm, foot, or leg under his opponent's arm or any body part.

Switch: This takes place when one grappler works to escape an inferior position and gain control, or at least get to a neutral position.

Takedown: Any move where the grappler takes his opponent from a standing position to the mat with the primary reason to gain further control of the opponent.

Third Arm: The third arm is the head. A grappler uses his head like it's a third arm to control his opponent.

Throw: Any move or skill where one grappler takes his opponent to the mat with control and force with the intention of ending the fight.

Tie-Up Leg or Foot: The leg or foot a grappler or fighter uses to form a triangle after the anchor leg has initially hooked an opponent's head, shoulder, or arm. The anchor leg initially controls the opponent and the tie-up leg connects to the anchor leg to form the triangle.

Time Hold: A term first coined (to our knowledge) by Gene LeBell. A time hold is any controlling position, hold, pin, or ride that is intended to control an opponent for a specified period of time to gain a victory or to gain

points. A time hold is useful in controlling an opponent for as long as necessary before applying a finishing hold or submission technique.

Top Fighting: In groundwork, the grappler who is on top. Often, grapplers who work from positions such as the top (spiral) ride, rodeo ride, or other positions that are not below or under the opponent.

Top Fighter or Top Grappler: The grappler or fighter who is on the top in groundfighting or ground grappling. This is also a term for a grappler who prefers to fight from the top position.

Transition: Any move or skill where one grappler takes his opponent to the mat, often immediately placing him in a finishing hold.

Trap: Any time a grappler uses his arms, hands, feet, legs, or any body part to grab, catch, and control an opponent's arm, hand, foot, leg, or any body part, that is a trap.

Wedge: Placing a body part to control an opponent. An example is a "head wedge" when one grappler places his head on his opponent's chest or shoulder to control the opponent.

Wrench: A wrench is the same as a crank. The point is to bend, twist, or force a joint out of its normal range of motion or movement.

ABOUT THE AUTHOR

Steve Scott has decades of training and coaching in judo, sambo, and jujitsu. He holds an eighth dan in judo, a seventh dan in Shingitai jujitsu, and is a member of the U.S. Sambo Hall of Fame. As a coach, he has developed hundereds of national and international medal winners as well as members of the world, Pan American, and Olympic teams. Steve has served as U.S. team coach at the World (under twenty-one) Judo Championships, Pan American Games for sambo, Pan American Championships for judo, World Sambo Championships, International High School Judo Championships, and numerous other international judo, sambo, and sport jujitsu events. Steve Scott lives in Kansas City, Missouri, with his wife Becky and their cats.

OTHER BOOKS BY STEVE SCOTT

The Judo Advantage: Controlling Movement with Modern Kinesiology, YMAA Publication Center, 2018

The Juji Gatame Encyclopedia: Comprehensive Applications of the Cross-Body Armlock, YMAA Publication Center, 2019

The Sambo Encyclopedia: Comprehensive Throws, Holds, and Submission Techniques, YMAA Publication Center, 2019

BOOKS FROM YMAA

101 REFLECTIONS ON TAI CHI CHUAN
108 INSIGHTS INTO TAI CHI CHUAN
A WOMAN'S QIGONG GUIDE
ADVANCING IN TAE KWON DO
ANALYSIS OF SHAOLIN CHIN NA 2ND ED
ANCIENT CHINESE WEAPONS
ART AND SCIENCE OF STAFF FIGHTING
THE ART AND SCIENCE OF SELF-DEFENSE
ART AND SCIENCE OF STICK FIGHTING
ART OF HOJO UNDO
ARTHRITIS RELIEF, 3D ED.
BACK PAIN RELIEF, 2ND ED.
BAGUAZHANG, 2ND ED.
BRAIN FITNESS
CHIN NA IN GROUND FIGHTING
CHINESE FAST WRESTLING
CHINESE FITNESS
CHINESE TUI NA MASSAGE
COMPLETE MARTIAL ARTIST
COMPREHENSIVE APPLICATIONS OF SHAOLIN CHIN NA
CONFLICT COMMUNICATION
DAO DE JING: A QIGONG INTERPRETATION
DAO IN ACTION
DEFENSIVE TACTICS
DIRTY GROUND
DR. WU'S HEAD MASSAGE
ESSENCE OF SHAOLIN WHITE CRANE
EXPLORING TAI CHI
FACING VIOLENCE
FIGHT LIKE A PHYSICIST
THE FIGHTER'S BODY
FIGHTER'S FACT BOOK 1&2
FIGHTING ARTS
FIGHTING THE PAIN RESISTANT ATTACKER
FIRST DEFENSE
FORCE DECISIONS: A CITIZENS GUIDE
INSIDE TAI CHI
JUDO ADVANTAGE
JUJI GATAME ENCYCLOPEDIA
KARATE SCIENCE
KATA AND THE TRANSMISSION OF KNOWLEDGE
KRAV MAGA COMBATIVES
KRAV MAGA FUNDAMENTAL STRATEGIES
KRAV MAGA PROFESSIONAL TACTICS
KRAV MAGA WEAPON DEFENSES
LITTLE BLACK BOOK OF VIOLENCE
LIUHEBAFA FIVE CHARACTER SECRETS
MARTIAL ARTS OF VIETNAM
MARTIAL ARTS INSTRUCTION
MARTIAL WAY AND ITS VIRTUES
MEDITATIONS ON VIOLENCE
MERIDIAN QIGONG EXERCISES
MINDFUL EXERCISE
MIND INSIDE TAI CHI
MIND INSIDE YANG STYLE TAI CHI CHUAN
NATURAL HEALING WITH QIGONG
NORTHERN SHAOLIN SWORD, 2ND ED.
OKINAWA'S COMPLETE KARATE SYSTEM: ISSHIN RYU
PRINCIPLES OF TRADITIONAL CHINESE MEDICINE
PROTECTOR ETHIC
QIGONG FOR HEALTH & MARTIAL ARTS 2ND ED.
QIGONG FOR TREATING COMMON AILMENTS

QIGONG MASSAGE
QIGONG MEDITATION: EMBRYONIC BREATHING
QIGONG GRAND CIRCULATION
QIGONG MEDITATION: SMALL CIRCULATION
QIGONG, THE SECRET OF YOUTH: DA MO'S CLASSICS
REDEMPTION
ROOT OF CHINESE QIGONG, 2ND ED.
SAMBO ENCYCLOPEDIA
SCALING FORCE
SELF-DEFENSE FOR WOMEN
SHIN GI TAI: KARATE TRAINING
SIMPLE CHINESE MEDICINE
SIMPLE QIGONG EXERCISES FOR HEALTH, 3RD ED.
SIMPLIFIED TAI CHI CHUAN, 2ND ED.
SOLO TRAINING 1&2
SPOTTING DANGER BEFORE IT SPOTS YOU
SPOTTING DANGER BEFORE IT SPOTS YOUR KIDS
SPOTTING DANGER BEFORE IT SPOTS YOUR TEENS
SUMO FOR MIXED MARTIAL ARTS
SUNRISE TAI CHI
SURVIVING ARMED ASSAULTS
TAE KWON DO: THE KOREAN MARTIAL ART
TAEKWONDO BLACK BELT POOMSAE
TAEKWONDO: A PATH TO EXCELLENCE
TAEKWONDO: ANCIENT WISDOM
TAEKWONDO: DEFENSE AGAINST WEAPONS
TAEKWONDO: SPIRIT AND PRACTICE
TAI CHI BALL QIGONG: FOR HEALTH AND MARTIAL ARTS
THE TAI CHI BOOK
TAI CHI CHIN NA, 2ND ED.
TAI CHI CHUAN CLASSICAL YANG STYLE, 2ND ED.
TAI CHI CHUAN MARTIAL POWER, 3RD ED.
TAI CHI CONCEPTS AND EXPERIMENTS
TAI CHI CONNECTIONS
TAI CHI DYNAMICS
TAI CHI FOR DEPRESSION
TAI CHI IN 10 WEEKS
TAI CHI PUSH HANDS
TAI CHI QIGONG, 3RD ED.
TAI CHI SECRETS OF THE ANCIENT MASTERS
TAI CHI SECRETS OF THE WU & LI STYLES
TAI CHI SECRETS OF THE WU STYLE
TAI CHI SECRETS OF THE YANG STYLE
TAI CHI SWORD: CLASSICAL YANG STYLE, 2ND ED.
TAI CHI SWORD FOR BEGINNERS
TAI CHI WALKING
TAIJIQUAN THEORY OF DR. YANG, JWING-MING
FIGHTING ARTS
TRADITIONAL CHINESE HEALTH SECRETS
TRADITIONAL TAEKWONDO
TRAINING FOR SUDDEN VIOLENCE
TRIANGLE HOLD ENCYCLOPEDIA
TRUE WELLNESS SERIES (MIND, HEART, GUT)
WARRIOR'S MANIFESTO
WAY OF KATA
WAY OF SANCHIN KATA
WAY TO BLACK BELT
WESTERN HERBS FOR MARTIAL ARTISTS
WILD GOOSE QIGONG
WINNING FIGHTS
XINGYIQUAN

AND MANY MORE . . .

VIDEOS FROM YMAA

ANALYSIS OF SHAOLIN CHIN NA
BAGUA FOR BEGINNERS 1 & 2
BAGUAZHANG: EMEI BAGUAZHANG
BEGINNER QIGONG FOR WOMEN 1 & 2
BEGINNER TAI CHI FOR HEALTH
CHEN TAI CHI CANNON FIST
CHEN TAI CHI FIRST FORM
CHEN TAI CHI FOR BEGINNERS
CHIN NA IN-DEPTH SERIES
FACING VIOLENCE: 7 THINGS A MARTIAL ARTIST MUST KNOW
FIVE ANIMAL SPORTS
FIVE ELEMENTS ENERGY BALANCE
INFIGHTING
INTRODUCTION TO QI GONG FOR BEGINNERS
JOINT LOCKS
KNIFE DEFENSE
KUNG FU BODY CONDITIONING 1 & 2
KUNG FU FOR KIDS AND TEENS SERIES
LOGIC OF VIOLENCE
MERIDIAN QIGONG
NEIGONG FOR MARTIAL ARTS
NORTHERN SHAOLIN SWORD
QI GONG 30-DAY CHALLENGE
QI GONG FOR ANXIETY
QI GONG FOR ARMS, WRISTS, AND HANDS
QIGONG FOR BEGINNERS: FRAGRANCE
QI GONG FOR BETTER BALANCE
QI GONG FOR BETTER BREATHING
QI GONG FOR CANCER
QI GONG FOR DEPRESSION
QI GONG FOR ENERGY AND VITALITY
QI GONG FOR HEADACHES
QI GONG FOR THE HEALTHY HEART
QI GONG FOR HEALTHY JOINTS
QI GONG FOR HIGH BLOOD PRESSURE
QIGONG FOR LONGEVITY
QI GONG FOR STRONG BONES
QI GONG FOR THE UPPER BACK AND NECK
QIGONG FOR WOMEN WITH DAISY LEE
QIGONG FLOW FOR STRESS & ANXIETY RELIEF
QIGONG MASSAGE
QIGONG MINDFULNESS IN MOTION
QI GONG—THE SEATED WORKOUT
QIGONG: 15 MINUTES TO HEALTH
SABER FUNDAMENTAL TRAINING
SAI TRAINING AND SEQUENCES
SANCHIN KATA: TRADITIONAL TRAINING FOR KARATE POWER
SCALING FORCE
SEARCHING FOR SUPERHUMANS
SHAOLIN KUNG FU FUNDAMENTAL TRAINING 1 & 2
SHAOLIN LONG FIST KUNG FU BEGINNER—INTERMEDIATE—
    ADVANCED SERIES
SHAOLIN SABER: BASIC SEQUENCES
SHAOLIN STAFF: BASIC SEQUENCES
SHAOLIN WHITE CRANE GONG FU BASIC TRAINING SERIES
SHUAI JIAO: KUNG FU WRESTLING
SIMPLE QIGONG EXERCISES FOR HEALTH
SIMPLE QIGONG EXERCISES FOR ARTHRITIS RELIEF
SIMPLE QIGONG EXERCISES FOR BACK PAIN RELIEF
SIMPLIFIED TAI CHI CHUAN: 24 & 48 POSTURES
SIMPLIFIED TAI CHI FOR BEGINNERS 48
SIX HEALING SOUNDS
SUN TAI CHI

SWORD: FUNDAMENTAL TRAINING
TAEKWONDO KORYO POOMSAE
TAI CHI BALL QIGONG SERIES
TAI CHI BALL WORKOUT FOR BEGINNERS
TAI CHI CHUAN CLASSICAL YANG STYLE
TAI CHI FIGHTING SET
TAI CHI FIT: 24 FORM
TAI CHI FIT: ALZHEIMER'S PREVENTION
TAI CHI FIT: CANCER PREVENTION
TAI CHI FIT FOR VETERANS
TAI CHI FIT: FOR WOMEN
TAI CHI FIT: FLOW
TAI CHI FIT: FUSION BAMBOO
TAI CHI FIT: FUSION FIRE
TAI CHI FIT: FUSION IRON
TAI CHI FIT: HEALTHY BACK SEATED WORKOUT
TAI CHI FIT: HEALTHY HEART WORKOUT
TAI CHI FIT IN PARADISE
TAI CHI FIT: OVER 50
TAI CHI FIT OVER 50: BALANCE EXERCISES
TAI CHI FIT OVER 50: SEATED WORKOUT
TAI CHI FIT OVER 60: GENTLE EXERCISES
TAI CHI FIT OVER 60: HEALTHY JOINTS
TAI CHI FIT OVER 60: LIVE LONGER
TAI CHI FIT: STRENGTH
TAI CHI FIT: TO GO
TAI CHI FOR WOMEN
TAI CHI FUSION: FIRE
TAI CHI QIGONG
TAI CHI PUSHING HANDS SERIES
TAI CHI SWORD: CLASSICAL YANG STYLE
TAI CHI SWORD FOR BEGINNERS
TAI CHI SYMBOL: YIN YANG STICKING HANDS
TAIJI & SHAOLIN STAFF: FUNDAMENTAL TRAINING
TAIJI CHIN NA IN-DEPTH
TAIJI 37 POSTURES MARTIAL APPLICATIONS
TAIJI SABER CLASSICAL YANG STYLE
TAIJI WRESTLING
TRAINING FOR SUDDEN VIOLENCE
UNDERSTANDING QIGONG SERIES
WATER STYLE FOR BEGINNERS
WHITE CRANE HARD & SOFT QIGONG
YANG TAI CHI FOR BEGINNERS
YOQI: MICROCOSMIC ORBIT QIGONG
YOQI QIGONG FOR A HAPPY HEART
YOQI:QIGONG FLOW FOR HAPPY MIND
YOQI:QIGONG FLOW FOR INTERNAL ALCHEMY
YOQI QIGONG FOR HAPPY SPLEEN & STOMACH
YOQI QIGONG FOR HAPPY KIDNEYS
YOQI QIGONG FLOW FOR HAPPY LUNGS
YOQI QIGONG FLOW FOR STRESS RELIEF
YOQI: QIGONG FLOW TO BOOST IMMUNE SYSTEM
YOQI SIX HEALING SOUNDS
YOQI: YIN YOGA 1
WU TAI CHI FOR BEGINNERS
WUDANG KUNG FU: FUNDAMENTAL TRAINING
WUDANG SWORD
WUDANG TAIJIQUAN
XINGYIQUAN
YANG TAI CHI FOR BEGINNERS

AND MANY MORE...

more products available from . . .

YMAA Publication Center, Inc. 楊氏東方文化出版中心

1-800-669-8892 • info@ymaa.com • www.ymaa.com

MARQUIS

Québec, Canada